How to Design & Build Storage Projects

Created and designed
by the editorial staff
of ORTHO Books

Project Editor	Sally W. Smith
Writer	Diane Snow Crocker
Designer	Michael Patrick Cronan
Illustrator	Edith Allgood
Photographer	Stephen Marley
Photographic Stylist	Sara Slavin
Construction Designs	Diane Snow Crocker

Ortho Books

Publisher
Robert L. Iacopi

Editorial Director
Min S. Yee

Managing Editor
Anne Coolman

Horticultural Editor
Michael D. Smith

Senior Editor
Kenneth R. Burke

Production Manager
Laurie Sheldon

Editors
Barbara J. Ferguson
Sally W. Smith

Horticulturists
Michael D. McKinley
Deni W. Stein

Production Assistant
Darcie S. Furlan

Editorial Assistants
Laurie A. Black
Anne D. Pederson
William F. Yusavage

National Sales Manager
Garry P. Wellman

Operations/Distribution
William T. Pletcher

Operations Assistant
Donna M. White

Administrative Assistant
Georgiann Wright

Address all inquiries to:
Ortho Books
Chevron Chemical Company
Consumer Products Division
575 Market Street
San Francisco, CA 94105

First Printing in April, 1983

1 2 3 4 5 6 7 8 9

83 84 85 86 87 88

ISBN 0-89721-017-4

Library of Congress Catalog Card
Number 82-63126

Chevron

Chevron Chemical Company
575 Market Street, San Francisco, CA 94105

Front Cover

You can transform even a
cramped closet into a well-
organized multipurpose storage
space when you fit it out with the
six-track system (see page 63).
This closet was designed to
include a vertical module, sized
to house drawerlike wire baskets
in stacking frames; a self-
supporting shelf; and door-back
fittings. See page 36 for another
look at this closet.

Back Cover

Four different approaches to
storage. Clockwise, starting at
top left, they are: stackable
modular cubes to buy—flexible
storage for any room (see page
46); tailor-made built-in
cabinetry—a combination of
cases and chests—easily
constructed to your own
specifications (see pages 74–77);
hooks and hangers, as attractive
as they are useful (see page 52);
an under-the-eaves desk—the
owner looked for more work and
storage space, and found it (see
page 19).

Page 1

Author Diane Snow Crocker
preceded her training in
architecture with woodshop
experience in building and
design.

Acknowledgments

See page 96

How to Design & Build Storage Projects

Looking for Space— and Finding It   5

Making Your Space Work for You   27

Instant Solutions: Storage Products You Can Buy   47

Tailor-Made Solutions: Storage Components You Can Build   59

Looking for Space— and Finding It

Storage starts with space, and chances are you've got more to work with than you realize. This chapter shows you how to find that space and how to use it well. Take the sixteen-page Photo Tour to see effective solutions to common storage problems.

Your storage situation needn't be a full-blown crisis to disrupt the pattern and rhythm of daily life. Whatever the scale of your storage problems, this book will help you identify their source—and solve the storage puzzle. You'll work with three key aspects of any storage situation: identifying the things you need to store and the places where they should be stored; seeing new ways to take advantage of your existing storage resources; and planning ways to tap unutilized storage potential by adding new components.

Storage starts with space. Finding space and making it work for you is what this book is all about. It offers a process that can help you get organized, ideas for fitting out your space with purchased storage aids, and techniques and directions for building storage projects from drawer dividers to wall systems. The result: a house-wide system that solves storage problems with efficiency and style.

How to Use This Book

Looking for Space—and Finding It. Chapter 1 focuses on the potential storage space that's hiding in your home. The illustration on pages 8 and 9 will help you look at your home as space, to see the places that can be utilized for storage. Then take the Photo Tour on pages 10 through 25 to see practical and attractive ways to make use of spaces of all sorts.

Making Your Space Work for You. Chapter 2 offers a five-step process for thinking through the way you use your space, before you build or buy a thing. Let the design guidelines on page 30 and the pointers on structure and style on pages 34 and 35 guide you as you organize your living space and design its storage system. The Potpourri of Project Ideas on pages 36 through 45 illustrates ways of combining components to plan a project that meets your needs.

Instant Solutions: Products You Can Buy. In Chapter 3 you'll find a brief survey of some of the storage helpers—from drawer inserts to furniture systems—that you can buy. These products can solve problems all by themselves, or they may be part of a project that you build.

Tailor-Made Solutions: Projects You Can Build. For truly individualized storage, there's nothing like the project you design to suit your particular situation. Chapter 4 contains instructions for building and adapting a range of basic storage components, along with a handbook on tools, workshop techniques, and tips. When you build it yourself, you're sure to get just what you want, and you'll have the satisfaction of living with your own craftsmanship.

A dining-room wall becomes a storage area with the addition of shelf-in-case units. The cubes are actually four separate cases with fixed shelves; where the top case fits onto the bottom one, interlocking rabbets help stabilize the stack. Oversized books fit well into the cubes, which are sturdy enough to hold the weight. Above, the open spaces show off the family's collections. The dining room gains not only practical storage but also a lively and colorful focal point.

A Perspective on Storage

Storage means more than just places to stow things. It's a system composed of three interrelated elements: people—those who need to get to and use stored things; places—the space devoted to storage functions; and things—the items stored. The better these three elements fit together, the better your storage system will work. This book is designed to help.

Where Storage Problems Begin

We all face storage problems. They arise from the structure of our homes and from the patterns of our lives. Most homes lack adequate storage facilities, possibly because storage space is rarely a priority when they're designed. Even when a home contains good storage space, individual life-styles will make a difference in how fully it is utilized. For example, older homes may have a built-in storage and serving space in a dining area, appropriate to an era of formal dining. Today's more casual lifestyle may well mean that such a unit is rarely used.

Individual living patterns can be at cross-purposes to the fundamental structure of the dwelling, as well, which will aggravate storage problems. Furniture arrangements and habits of doing certain tasks in certain places may conflict with the natural traffic paths and activity areas of a home; such a conflict undermines even dogged attempts at improving storage—or anything else (traffic patterns and activity areas are discussed on pages 28–31).

It is also a fact that, over the years, we tend to have more and more possessions. Households expand in the twinkling of an eye, but the size of living space doesn't. Perhaps it's a new baby—complete with diapers, highchair, and stroller. Perhaps it's children who grow into and then out of everything—clothing, activities, toys—faster than seems possible. Or maybe your own changing interests bring a tide of new things into your life: board games, expanding libraries and record collections, or new hobby, cooking, and sports equipment. Somehow there are more things that we can't live without, such as food processors, video equipment, televisions, tape cassette players, and hair dryers. In addition, there are the cherished mementoes of a lifetime, family heirlooms, and personal records—all of which have to be dealt with somehow.

Getting Started on Solutions

Your own storage situation will be unique. People differ; no two households are quite alike; even identical dwellings will be used quite differently by different people. The particular way in which you approach and resolve your own storage problems will be appropriate for you. There is no single rule or set of rules that will apply to every situation, but there are some basic approaches that can help you untangle even the tightest storage knots.

One thing to keep in mind is that, although to have a storage system you need to be systematic—that is, to be logical and organized—you can make up your own system. Some people find it very sensible to store spices in alphabetical order; some do the same with their books. Perhaps alphabetical order doesn't work for you, especially in your kitchen. That's fine; but you'll want to find some way to organize your books and spices that you *will* be comfortable with. You may want to group items by size or shape—all the frying pans on one shelf—or by frequency of use—the two frying pans you always use in a handy place, two others in a less-accessible spot. You may want everything of one kind together—all good coats, hats, and boots in the entryway closet, all rough or dirty outerwear hanging on hooks in the back hall—or you may want items used by particular individuals collected together—all adult coats, boots, and hats in the entryway, all kids' things out back. None of these methods of organizing is necessarily best; what's important is that there *is* a method. When part of the process of improving your storage situation is to settle on a method, then you have a framework to fall back on every time you look at an object and wonder where you'll put it. If at some point the method seems to be losing its effectiveness, it may be time to reevaluate it and establish a new method.

Keeping current is a key issue in any storage situation. We change over time, as do our interests and activities. We sometimes forget to change our living spaces to match our lives. Often a storage problem develops because we've outgrown some interest, but never quite gotten rid of its related equipment. For instance, in basements and garages all across the continent there repose outgrown skis and old wooden tennis racquets. Many homes have formal living rooms that amount to wasted space because entertaining takes place in the family room. Or a house may have a nice little sewing area that is no longer well-utilized space because other activities have replaced sewing. One way to start on storage improvements is just to review the pattern of daily life and see what changes have occurred.

Finally, keep a sense of proportion about the subject. Your storage problems may be driving you to despair, and solving them is important, but a rigidly organized, inflexibly ruled home won't be a happy or satisfactory solution.

At its heart, the aim of improving storage is to decrease the amount of attention it requires. If you can get the pedestrian aspects of daily life to chug cheerfully along as a self-sustaining support system, it will free you and those you share life with for more engaging activities. Storage begins with space; it can end with people—living in balance with one another and their surroundings.

People and Places

As you think about changes and improvements in your storage system, you have an opportunity to arrange your living space so that it fully serves the people who use it. You and those who share your home come in different sizes and shapes, with different physical characteristics, strengths, and abilities. Standard building practices can't take individual physical needs into detailed account; for the sake of economy, homes are built for an average consumer. For instance, standard kitchen counters are 36 inches high. Yet the people who use them might be much more comfortable if they were lowered to 32 inches, or raised to 40 inches. When you're purchasing or building improvements for your home, you can make such adjustments.

The illustrations on this page show some of the factors to take into consideration. For example, how high and how far can you comfortably reach? What about your children, and their grandparents? How low can any of you comfortably bend? What are the differences in your lines of sight? Do any of you have mobility limitations? You may find it helpful to keep a list of measurements describing the ranges of motion of those in your household. Use it as a reference when you're deciding on dimensions for additions and improvements to your storage or your living space.

Consider also the space you allow for circulation and work zones. Any work zone such as the kitchen stove needs a clear area in which a person can stand, bend over, move from side to side. This zone can impinge on an adjacent circulation zone, or traffic pathway; people aren't walking there all the time. The circulation zone in itself should be at least wide enough for a person to walk comfortably through it. Keep these considerations in mind so that you don't build yourself into a congested corner.

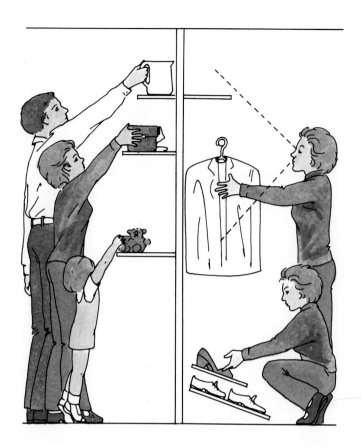

Finding Space

The drawing at right points out some spaces in a typical home that may be unused or under-used, and suggests some ways, drawn from the photographs and illustrations in this book, that storage potential can be tapped. Consider the ideas shown here and throughout this book, read through the guidelines below, and then look at your home with new eyes to find the space you need.

Start by examining the storage areas you now have to see if you can utilize them better. Only when you've used all existing space to best advantage should you consider new construction. In looking for places to add storage capacity, search out the nooks, insets, gaps, next-tos (next to the door, next to the stove), spots above or below existing units such as a refrigerator, places that can be filled in and fitted out without sacrificing a lot of floor space. Don't forget that you can build into the space between studs on interior walls.

Look at all surfaces. A door back can be lined with pockets (see pages 64–65). In some places—the garage, basement, attic, or laundry room, for instance—door fronts can also be put to work: hooks and racks can be fastened on them, or they can be surfaced with perforated board.

Look at all volumes. Seating units, for instance, always enclose a space that might be a storage place. Build a couch above pull-out drawers, add a window seat, or turn a storage cube into a seat by topping it with a cushion. There's a lot of volume under a staircase.

Examine your own "musts." Do you have to have a dresser? You may be able to substitute enough shelves, baskets, and pockets to do without one. Does your "dining room" have to be used for dining? It might be better utilized as a study, with a dining table in the living room instead.

Consider ways that you can make any space serve more than one function; that will free another part of the house. Can the cookbook corner of the kitchen become an all-purpose desk? Can your work space—sewing, typing, model

airplanes—be a cube on wheels that tucks into a corner or closet, so you needn't devote space full-time to a use that's only part-time?

Think, too, about the structure of the house and your household's needs. Would you like a more open space, or set-apart, specialized areas; more privacy, or more togetherness? Can you add a room divider with storage in it? Can you eliminate furniture?

On the following pages is a Photo Tour of Storage Spaces; the ideas shown there can aid you in the process of developing a new awareness of the storage potential in your home.

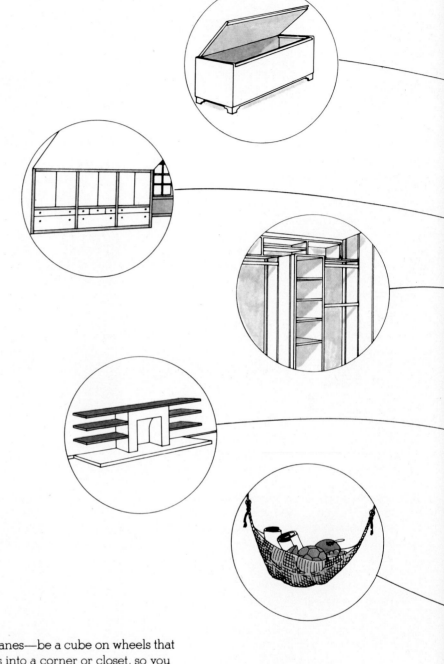

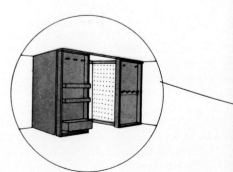

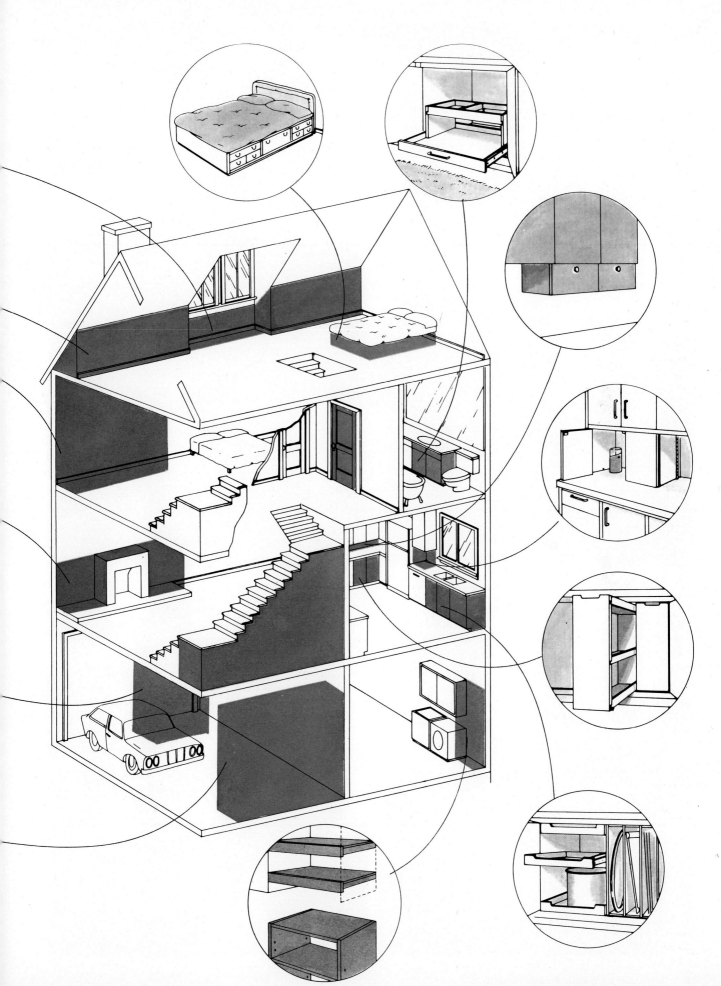

A Photo Tour of Storage Spaces

Bathroom storage is usually just a set of cabinets. You can increase their capacity by installing a horizontal rollout shelf under the sink, as shown on the opposite page at top. The rollout allows you to reach bulky items at the rear of the cabinet without disturbing small things in the front. For other rollout configurations, see pages 70–71.

Deep drawers fitted with dividers make ideal storage for pots, pans, and lids. Slip them between vertical dividers spaced according to their sizes. The drawer opposite (left below) does the job of two full-depth base cabinet shelves, yet consumes only half the amount of storage space. It is mounted on full-extension, heavy-duty slides.

Platform rollouts can replace standard base cabinetry shelves. Mounted on full-extension, heavy-duty slides, as shown opposite (right below), they can carry a great deal of weight. The full-extension slides allow tighter packing and even stacking of stored things—and since you need allow only a few inches of headspace between the rollouts, you can have five or six surfaces where the average cabinet has only two.

A handy little phone spot puts address and telephone books right where you need them—and hides them behind a fold-down door when you're through. The fold-down surface is large enough to open the book on and sturdy enough to support it.

Metal-lined bucket drawers hold flour and sugar ready for easy scooping. Like the other ideas shown on these two pages, these drawers maximize the use of below-counter space, and free countertops for other functions. In a kitchen where pests are not a problem, drawers such as these can hold any bulk supplies.

A Photo Tour of Storage Spaces

Open shelves combine access and aesthetics in a very pleasant way. In the top photograph at left are two variations. The owner of the kitchen prefers closed cupboards for most of his storage, but added one open shelf at the bottom of the cabinets for frequently used items. Then he topped the backsplash with a narrow shelf to hold the odds and ends that often clutter working surfaces—salt and pepper shakers, garlic, some spices, and fruit—plus a pair of pictures. The result: an easy-to-use, well-ordered kitchen that is warmed by personal touches.

A case of shelves can mount against a wall or hang from the ceiling, expanding storage capacity without subtracting floor or cabinet space. Open shelves such as the two examples shown at the bottom of the opposite page can house attractive daily-use dinnerware and glassware. Like art, handsome cooking and serving dishes bring warmth and visual interest to a room. Because the pieces are used frequently, the arrangement is easy to keep clean and in order. The result is both practical and good-looking.

Vertical rollouts can replace base cabinets to maximize usable storage space. On the rollout below left, a large load of kitchen appliances and equipment glides out into the open kitchen space, where the items can be seen, reached, used, and put away with ease. Mounted on heavy-duty full-extension slides, the rollout pulls out of the side of a sink island, and has an adjacent electrical outlet ready for use. The bottom shelf is fixed to lend rigidity to the unit; the upper two are adjustable. At right below, a double-shelf vertical rollout makes good use of a narrow cabinet space. This vertical rollout is also mounted on heavy-duty full-extension slides. It has the added feature of a built-in food processor mechanism, permanently wired through the back of the case, at a convenient height for use. The rollout is topped with an easy-to-clean, durable plastic-laminate work surface. Such an installation keeps counter surfaces clear for work, without sacrificing convenience. Note that narrow lips on the double-access shelves hold the contents safely in place, but don't hamper removal or replacement of stored items.

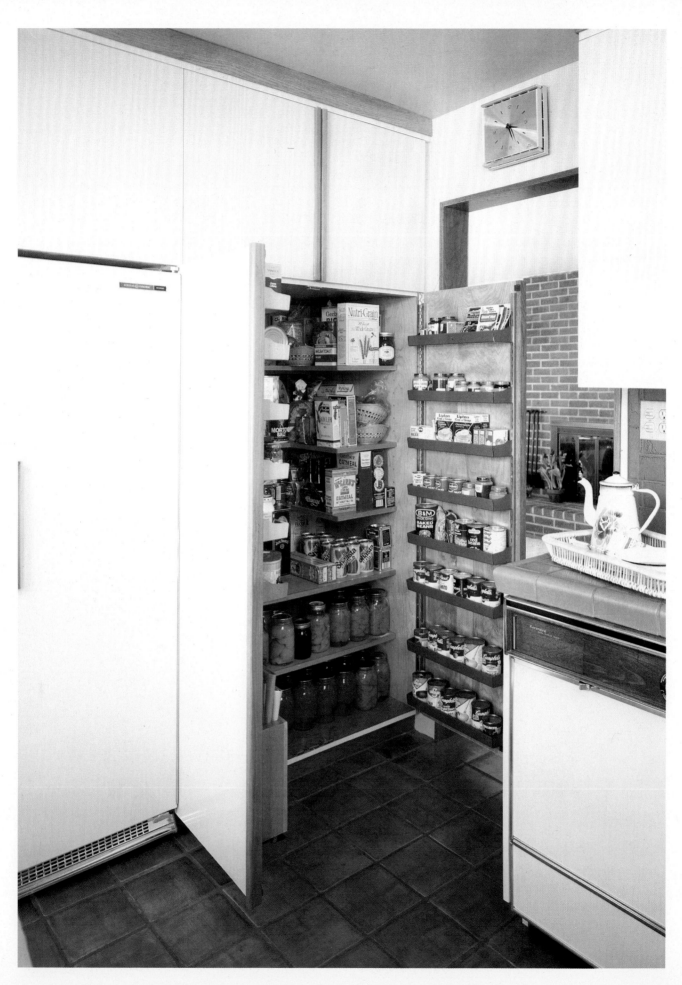

A Photo Tour of Storage Spaces

A pantry is a wonderful thing! The one shown at left has double doors that swing wide to open the whole interior to view. Planning a menu, making up a grocery list, hunting for a snack are easy endeavors with such a well-arranged cabinet. It combines built-in shelves with purchased door-back pockets, their height adjusted to coincide with the gaps between the shelves. The upper shelves are cut away for greater convenience in reaching the goods stored on them. Note the careful proportions of the pantry: it is the same depth and height as the refrigerator next to it, carrying the vertical wall plane and the horizontal height line smoothly across to the adjacent wall.

A case of shelves can become a door, or vice versa. The lumber bookcase below left covers one side of a door that is sturdily fastened with heavy-duty continuous hinge to the adjacent wall framing. Precisely because the unit is heavy, its arc of swing is smooth and sure, keeping the contents of the shelves secure during travel. The case was carefully sized to have sufficient clearance to close. Mounted flush with the hinge-side wall, it can open a full 180 degrees. Since its shelves are at the same intervals as the neighboring ones, when it is closed, the door becomes part of a continuous wall of bookcases.

Niches are easy to frame into any wall that covers a space or void—between studs, in no-longer-used ducts or vents, or, as in the photograph below right, next to a fireplace flue. In this instance, the owner installed a prefabricated fireplace. Rather than just cover over the volume to either side of the insulated sheet-metal flue, he sized three niches on each side of the fireplace framing to hold art books and special objects. Framed, sheathed with wallboard, and trimmed, the niches are a useful small addition to storage space that is in keeping with the style of the room. A similar kind of framing will create a boxed space (called a soffit) in any area, such as above a refrigerator.

A Photo Tour of Storage Spaces

This young man's closet is a tailor-made conversion of a standard double-width sliding-door closet. The designer halved the space by installing a vertical divider that supports one end of the closet rod. The divider, the opposite side wall, and the back wall are lined with narrow wood slats. Broom hangers hold hats, shoes, sports equipment, and other hangable items, and are easy to reposition as storage needs change. Because boys' and men's clothing stores efficiently on half-height closet rods, the pole was hung low.

A child's play and storage space was tucked into half of an L-shaped closet in this small room. The L has a pair of clothes rods, one low enough for the child to reach. The modular drawer unit with seat cushion on top holds clothing. On the shelves above, washtubs corral small toy pieces, and the stuffed animals are just a climb-up away. As the child's wardrobe expands and his play patterns change, the space can be easily converted to more conventional closet use.

Girl's closet (opposite) features a built-in bank of drawers flanked by vertical dividers to which tracks have been attached. The rods have been mounted at a height appropriate to a growing teenager; shelves could be added at any level along the tracks. This flexible system makes it possible to use all the interior space of the closet and to adapt it to changing needs.

A Photo Tour of Storage Spaces

Attics and under-the-eaves areas contain a wealth of usable space. The workroom shown on the opposite page was created for a designer-writer. The wall-length work and desk area fits against the knee wall, where the ceiling is low; the cutting table extends well out into the room, where headroom is ample. Supported by a double-sided cabinet-and-drawer unit in which fabric, patterns, and other supplies are stored, the cutting table is convenient for either standing or sitting on the tall stools.

The under-the-eaves desk at right makes good use of space where standing room is limited. This 4-foot by 11-foot area, previously an inefficient closet, becomes a quiet and functional workspace with the installation of file-size drawer units under a plastic-laminate desktop.

The attic bedroom at bottom contains only a bed—all the rest of the "furniture" is built in. Against the knee wall, a chest of drawers comes up to the line of the windowsill. The height of the end wall allows a bank of walk-in closets, one of which is shown. The bookshelf under the window has a top sturdy enough to supply a sitting surface in this room without furniture.

A Photo Tour of Storage Spaces

A stair landing (left below) afforded a special opportunity for storage space adjacent to the kitchen. A built-in wine rack houses a considerable number of bottles out of the way but conveniently accessible. Beneath that, the security system sits behind sliding doors; there's no need to look at the equipment except when you want to. Big doors below cover the stereo components and large, bulky items—in this central location they're handy to most of the house. The unit is made of the same wood as the cabinets in the nearby kitchen, which creates a visual link between the two areas.

A hideaway bar accommodates soda pop, liquor, wines, hors d'oeuvre trays, cocktail napkins, and an assortment of glassware all in one small corner. There's plenty of storage space here, as well as a sink and an undercounter refrigerator. Bi-folding doors are painted to match the adjacent living room cabinetry. Like the cabinetry, they extend floor to ceiling, carrying a continuous horizontal line at the ceiling and floor. This unifies the architectural elements of the room and creates a quiet, inviting effect.

Stereo components and other sound equipment can be housed in a tailored-to-fit closet. In the instance of the setup shown opposite, the owner of the home was willing to give up conventional closet space in order to gain a well-organized system for equipment, tapes, and albums. The shelving was sized to fit the items it holds. Heavy-duty, full-extension slides keep the turntable steady; speaker wires installed with the shelving run down through the closet floor and up to speakers in an adjacent room. The bi-folding louvered doors make an attractive exterior, behind which the music can play unattended.

A Photo Tour of Storage Spaces

A boy's bedroom triples as a working, playing, and sleeping area. A window-side work station houses a computer on a slide-out platform that brings the equipment forward and also allows access to the back of the unit. A roll-down tamboured door closes everything neatly away. The counter, supported by two deep-drawer chests that hold clothing, sports equipment, and toys, is set low to carry the horizontal line of the bed across to meet that of the window seat. Under the bed, a full-length, heavy-duty rollout drawer holds board games and large toys. The bookcase headboard provides space for both reference books and reading-in-bed material. On the left is one of three ladder-like units securely fastened to the wall. As shown, it is part of an exercise system; opened out, the units can be locked in place to support a series of shelves for books.

Modular cases compose an attractive storage system that can be arranged and rearranged in any number of configurations. The five modules shown here are matched by another five on the other side of the window; a set of smaller cases encloses more storage and forms a comfortable window seat at the same time. Smooth-lined flush inset doors cover most of the modules; inside, the modules accommodate bulky items or, on adjustable shelves, flat things like board games. The system is flexible, versatile, orderly, and designed with attention to detail: note that the cushions on the window seat match its height to that of the stacking modules, producing a smooth horizontal line just at windowsill level.

A mirrored wall is only part of the answer to the problem of a small room. In the 10-foot by 14-foot bedroom at right, the owner framed a door and filled the wall with shelves to hold art objects and books. Without the shelves, the room would be crowded with floor-standing furniture to hold these items. The uprights reach from floor to ceiling, helping to stretch the height of the room. The shelves are attached by an invisible method that lends a clean, uncluttered look to the room: A front edging of 2-inch lumber joins two pieces of 1/2-inch plywood; the gap between the plywood pieces, established by spacer blocks, allows the shelves to slide over fixed cleats. The result is a sturdy construction that doesn't reveal the secret of its support. The clean, simple lines of the storage wall, repeated in the blinds and bedspread, give the room a calm and restful appeal and also join with the mirrored walls to expand its apparent size.

This antique armoire still gives service as clothing storage, and finds a welcome place in the bedroom-study at right. The room itself is narrow; the piece is wide and deep. With careful attention to detail, the architect designed a storage wall that suits both the antique and the room. The nook, sized to hold the armoire so that its face is flush with the wall, integrates the piece into the room so that it neither overpowers it nor seems incongruous in the contemporary setting. At the same time, other spaces are created by the construction. The niches above display a collection of small art objects—they're clearly visible yet out of harm's way.

A Photo Tour of Storage Spaces

This cozy family room makes the most out of a window in a wall. The window seat is a storage chest; behind the center doors of the base cabinet is a television; and the side compartments include a drawer sized to hold record albums. Stereo components, toys and games, shelved books, pictures, and a tank of household pets all find a home here. The basis is simply case and chest construction. Design considerations include applied moldings and paint that matches the walls so that the unit blends into the existing architecture.

A dining area next to the kitchen is attractive and filled with storage capacity as well. On the left is a space-defining peninsula with a sink and work surface on the far side and bookshelves and a serving surface on the side seen here. On the end wall, cabinetry flanks the fireplace. The left bank of cabinets stores china and serving pieces. The right bank holds home office equipment and household records above the desk surface between the fireplace and the window. At the corner where the peninsula and the end wall meet, an appliance garage neatly encloses kitchen equipment behind a roll-down tamboured door. The chair at the head of the table can be turned around for use at the desk. Thus a relatively small space becomes a central family living area where a diversity of activities can take place.

Bookcase nooks that recess to either side of the marble-faced fireplace provide storage and also contribute to the harmony of a warm and welcoming room. To give an integrated effect to the whole wall, the heights of the cases continue the line of the mantle top, and the whole installation is trimmed with the same molding. The regular spacing of the shelves, combined with the balanced arrangement of the furniture, furthers the impression of serenity and calm. Above the shelves, the top surfaces of the mantel and cases provide considerable display space for a prized collection without creating either a crowded jumble or a museum effect. Echoing the ample proportions of the room, the uncramped scale of the storage wall provides generous shelf space and a unifying design element at the same time.

Making Your Space Work for You

Follow these Five Steps to Better Storage to improve your own system. Eight pages of illustrations show you a Potpourri of Project Ideas that will help you refine your scheme.

Making your space work for you means setting aside all the old notions of what storage is "supposed" to be so that you can take a fresh perspective on your existing space resources—both living areas and storage space.

Even if your storage problem seems to be limited to one area, such as the garage or perhaps just a closet, you'll want to think of that area in relationship to the other storage facilities in your home. Often a problem in one area aggravates the situation in other, seemingly unrelated areas as well; on the other hand, an improvement in one spot can have a beneficial impact elsewhere. For example, it may seem that a front-hall closet is for storing outerwear, if for no other reason than the dictates of tradition and habit. But your lifestyle and living patterns might lead you to redesign your closet to serve a variety of functions, as the one shown on the front cover does. That closet serves as much more than a place for the usual coats and boots. It comfortably accommodates the picnic basket, blanket, and binoculars, out of the way but still easy to reach; a small wine assortment; household tools, giftwrap and knitting supplies, briefcases and umbrellas; and sports equipment, duffled

and ready to go out the door. Storing these things here frees valuable space in other parts of the house.

The techniques described in this chapter constitute a process that will help you set up your own best storage system. The Five Steps to Better Storage start with an overview of your own home and its particular characteristics, so that you can arrange your furnishings to take advantage of them. The design guidelines on page 30 will help. Once this underlying structure is in place, the next step is to have a look at your storage methods and facilities, and the things you need to store. You may be able to accommodate your belongings simply by reorganizing them. Or you may find you need more storage space. If so, this process will guide you in determining how much space you need, where it's needed, what it will hold, and how you'd like it to work for you. Then, for some practical examples of ways to cure storage headaches, browse through the illustrated Potpourri of Project Ideas on pages 36 through 45.

In this chapter, the process of exploring and assessing a storage situation and creating an attractive, functional system for it is applied to a single room. However, the approach is effective at any scale—from a tangle in a drawer to a whole house. You may want to start with a small, defined space such as a closet. When you discover how easy it is to create a smooth-functioning system, and see how it dissolves problems in other areas, you may well decide to tackle every storage problem in your home.

Planning a better storage system starts with an assessment of your existing space and how you're using it. A tape measure, graph paper, a ruler, an eraser, and colored pencils can help you make a diagram that shows traffic patterns and activity areas. Put a little time into the planning stage and have fun with it; your overall storage system will be the better for it.

Five Steps to Better Storage

The five-step process described on these pages will help you solve the problem of clutter and overcrowding in any room in your house. The process entails

1. Discovering your traffic patterns and the activity areas they shape.
2. Coordinating your furniture arrangement with the traffic pattern.
3. Designing activity areas.
4. Figuring out what goes where.
5. Putting it away.

Looking at traffic patterns and activity areas shows you how the room itself is set up to function smoothly and well. Arranging the furniture to coordinate with traffic patterns will eliminate bumping, tripping, and congestion and encourage an easy flow through your room. Designing activity areas helps you choose where to locate and how to organize your activities. Figuring out what goes where shows you how to create a flexible and sensible storage system, whether it be for a drawer, a room, or a whole house. Putting it away implements your plan.

1. Discovering Traffic Patterns and Activity Areas

Traffic Patterns. First of all, see how the room itself is structured. The more you know about how your room works, the better you can make it work for you. Where are the doors—the entry and exit points? Where are the closets or built-in cabinetry? These elements are fixed; getting to and from them creates the natural traffic patterns in the room.

Even though you can't see them, these pathways may cause storage problems just as much as overcrowding does. If the routes to your storage places are congested or awkward to use, it may be too much trouble to put things away. By contrast, when you recognize your room's natural traffic patterns and arrange the furniture with respect to them, you create a harmony between the room itself and how you use it. And you may find that your storage problem isn't a shortage of space after all. You might simply need to adjust your furniture so that uncongested pathways aid you in using the existing storage capacity.

Activity Areas. If traffic patterns can be thought of as pathways, then activity areas are the dwelling places they connect. These areas house people—at least temporarily—and belongings. An activity area may be as small as a closet (the activity carried out there being storage) or it may be a large portion of a room— the conversation area around a fireplace, say, or a kitchen's work triangle (refrigerator to stove to sink).

Storage takes place in activity areas, not where traffic moves; defining activity areas is a first step to organizing a storage system.

Discovering your traffic patterns and activity areas is easy. All you do is map your space.

Mapping Your Space

■ Measure the space; start at one corner and work your way around the room, wall by wall, and sketch it to scale. Use graph paper to capture its proportions. Include door openings, windows, closets, and other built-in features. Place a piece of tracing paper over your sketch and trace the walls and doors.

■ Draw in the major traffic pathways—those you use most frequently—between entry and exit doors. With a lighter pencil line, draw the secondary traffic routes, such as those that go to built-in features. These are the room's natural traffic pathways, which shape its activity areas.

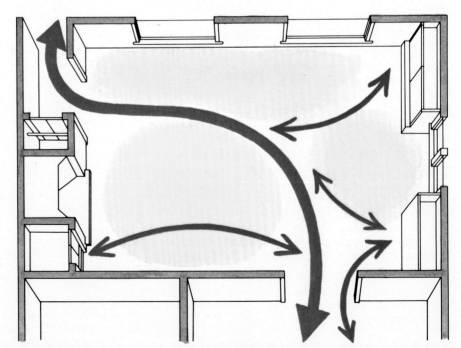

2. Coordinating Furniture with Traffic Patterns

Put a clean piece of tracing paper over your original sketch and retrace the walls and doors. Roughly sketch in the furniture as it is currently placed.

■ Now put the furniture plan over your traffic map. Does your furniture arrangement harmonize with the room's natural traffic patterns, or are there conflicts where traffic is blocked by furniture?

■ Use fresh tracing paper over your graph paper plan to sketch out various rearrangement schemes—even minor adjustments in furniture placement can make a tremendous difference in how the room looks, feels, and works. Work freely and quickly; you're just playing with ideas now.

Try to place furniture so that the major traffic path is obvious and easy to follow. For example, this might mean placing a table or work island in the kitchen in such a way that people walking from the back door to the hall naturally bypass the sink-stove-refrigerator work triangle.

Consider the characteristics of the furniture as well. You won't want a frequently used cupboard adjacent to a traffic path if it causes congestion. A drop-leaf table will work well in even a fairly narrow hallway—unless you often need to use the leaf. Remember that a desk chair isn't always snugged up against the desk; you should allow at least 2 feet (and preferably 3 feet) of clearance between the desk and a doorway. You may want to pull a piece of furniture into the middle of the room—that bookcase might make a great room divider—but check its back first. Sofa backs look

fine, but wood pieces frequently have unfinished backs.

Don't forget the utilitarian details. As you place the furniture, think about where the lighting will go. Is there an adjacent outlet or a safe and sensible path for an extension cord? Rewiring may not be in your budget. Can you place the phone where you need it? What about hooking up the television? If you have it on a movable stand, can it move smoothly between the places you'll want it?

As you work out a floor plan that defines and serves traffic paths and activity areas, refer to the design guidelines on page 30 for help in making it attractive as well as functional. Let all of your ideas coalesce into one or two tentative layouts—but don't actually move the furniture yet. First, design your activity areas, as described on page 31; this may call for some adjustments in your floor plan.

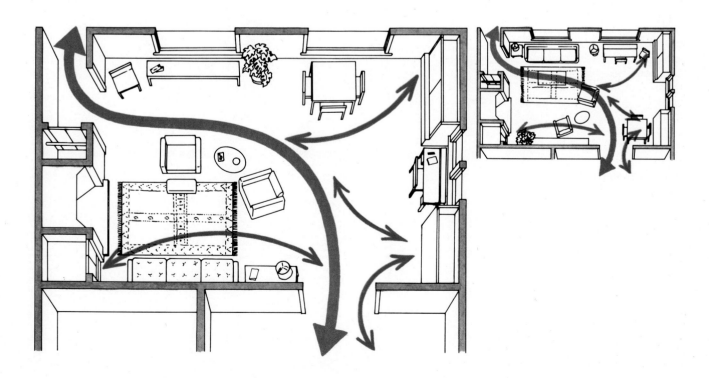

Five Steps to Better Storage

Guidelines on Design

These guidelines help you design your activity areas so that the room functions in an integrated way. The better your room works as a whole, the better the smaller systems—such as storage—will work within it. The three fundamental guidelines below apply to spatial design at every level of scale. Whether you're adding new furniture, building in a storage component, or simply rearranging an area, these principles will help you create a room as full of harmony and beauty as it is functional and efficient.

Closure and Connection.

When you arrange furniture, you can position pieces to define a space that traffic can flow around, not through. For instance, by placing a pair of armchairs with their backs at the edge of a traffic pathway, you can create an inviting conversation area. It seems special because the chairs create a sense of closure, but it doesn't feel walled off, since your line of sight maintains a connection with the rest of the room.

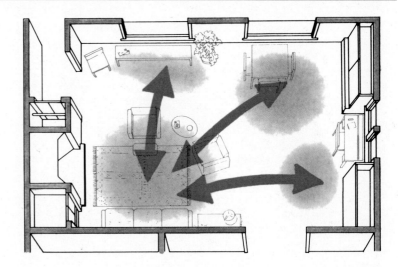

Height Lines.

As you arrange your room, consider the combined visual effect of the furniture's height lines. Every horizontal surface creates a visual line. These lines needn't be identical, but if furniture height lines rise and recede in a smooth, orderly way, you'll create a spacious, calm quality. Arbitrary, abrupt changes in height can create a jumpy and uncomfortable effect.

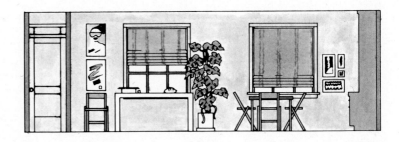

Architectural Reference Points.

Use vertical lines such as the edges of doors, windows, fireplaces, cabinetry, and nooks as reference points to help fine-tune your furniture arrangements. Imagine those edges projecting into the room to form a spatial grid, then see where you might be able to align furniture edges with that grid, or center pieces in areas formed by it. Chairs, tables, sofas, even area rugs knit securely with the space when you use the natural grid to create an underlying order in the room.

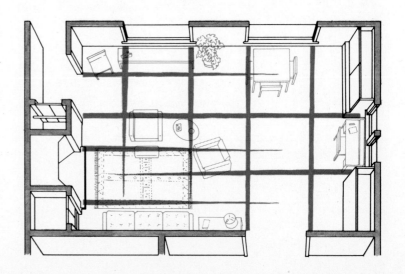

3. Designing Activity Areas

Often, what is perceived as a storage problem is actually an activity located in an inappropriate place. If you can resolve this conflict, chances are you'll also improve your storage situation at the same time.

For instance, is your iron permanently in "temporary" residence in the family room because you always iron in front of the television? Go ahead and make a home for the appliance in the cabinet next to the TV. Bring the ironing board out of exile while you're at it; at this point, don't worry how you'll accommodate it. Good storage puts things in the right place so they are accessible. This may not be the storage system the architect or your mother envisioned, but if you iron in front of the TV, why not make it easy to do so? You'll want to arrange your storage setup to reflect your own idea of the right place for things.

A floor plan with uncongested traffic paths and newly defined activity areas is the basis for the next step: clarifying what activity belongs in each area.

■ First, take a minute to analyze the room's characteristics. Different areas have qualities you'll want to take advantage of—natural light, a fireplace, a cozy nook, generous open space, a beautiful view—as well as some you'll want to circumvent, like appliance noise or a draft. Perhaps a quiet corner of the bedroom is the perfect place for writing letters and paying bills. Can you fit your desk there?

■ Now, list the different things you and your household members typically do in the room. Sort your list into categories—activities that are energetic or quiet, those that require some equipment versus those that don't, things done seated or standing, for example. Choose

categories that make the most sense for you. While you're at it, take a moment to dream a little. For each area, add to your activities list anything you might like to do there if the space could be made appropriate. For instance, you might have on your kitchen list just the usual food-related activities. Now you might add menu planning, children's homework, and flower arranging. Keep this "wish list" in mind as you continue the process. You may be surprised at how much of it you can move from dream to reality.

■ Now look to see if your activities are currently located in appropriate areas of the room. Placing an activity in an appropriate area means respecting the nature of the room—both its structure, as revealed by its traffic pattern, and its ambience, as defined by the special characteristics of the space. Be sure as you decide what activity goes where that you are working with, not against, the structure of the area and its ambience, or you will be unhappy with the result.

■ Compare your new floor plan with your list, and be prepared to adjust either the activities or the floor plan until they are harmonious. Do quiet activities share the same space as energetic ones? This is workable if they go on at separate times, but if they coincide, you have a conflict that you need to resolve. Is there sufficient space for group activities? If not, you need to relocate the activities or rework your scheme to expand that activity area.

When you think your floor plan is the best one for your activities and your household, rearrange the furniture. Then suspend your planning process for a few days while you live with the new arrangement and see if it suits you. Fine-tune it if necessary.

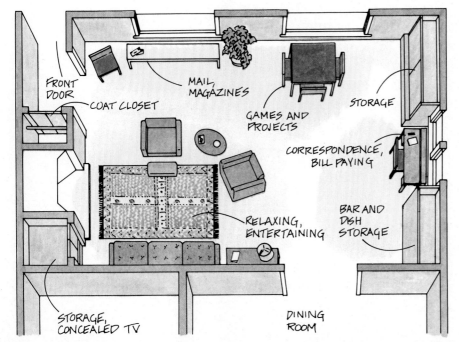

FRONT DOOR

COAT CLOSET

MAIL, MAGAZINES

GAMES AND PROJECTS

STORAGE

CORRESPONDENCE, BILL PAYING

RELAXING, ENTERTAINING

BAR AND DISH STORAGE

STORAGE, CONCEALED TV

DINING ROOM

Five Steps to Better Storage

4. Figuring Out What Goes Where

Now that you've thought through your activity areas, you're ready to tackle the question of what you want to store in them. First, look at the types of storage spaces you have in your newly arranged room. Assess each piece of furniture; what type of storage space does it offer? Does it have drawers; are they deep or shallow? Does it have shelves; are they adjustable? Next, look at the things that are stored in your existing units. Does it make sense to store those things there? Use the guidelines on these pages to create and implement a new storage plan that utilizes your existing storage spaces well and allocates your belongings among them in the most sensible way. If your plan calls for new storage facilities, use Chapters 3 and 4 to select the appropriate ones.

Getting organized can actually be fun. History—both ancient and recent—replays itself before your eyes as your closet or storage units yield up those relics, old favorites, and forgotten items, many of which bear no relationship to your current life.

Take a visual inventory.

■ Across the top of a sheet of paper, list the activities you plan for the area at hand.
■ Under each activity, list everything you need or would like to have nearby.
■ Draw a big, bold line across the page underneath your list.
■ Open all the doors and drawers of the storage units in the area. What's inside?
■ Check off the things above the line that are already in the storage unit.
■ Below the line, list all the other things you find in the unit.
■ Whatever you don't find but need, circle. Go get those things; you'll want to have them there.

Take a look at all the "stuff" on your list below the line. Are these the

"right" things in the "wrong" place? If so, put them where they belong. Or, are they simply no longer "right" things, things you no longer care to keep? To help you decide, answer the following questions and then make your choice: Is it damaged or broken—and not likely to get fixed? Can you remember when you last used it? Do you like it anymore? Do you have and use something else instead? Would someone else like to receive or buy it? Are you keeping it only in case someday you need it (or you get thin again, or it comes back into style)?

Trade your problem for a solution.

When you've cornered the culprit—that mountain of things you needn't store at all—consider your options. You could just throw it away, but you could also:

■ Convert it to cash through garage sales or a newspaper ad. If you're disposing of furniture, or anything a bit old, or something you think might have value, offer it to an antique or second-hand store or auction house. Or let someone else do the selling for you: thrift shops run by charitable organizations will take many items and send you a receipt for your tax-deductible contribution.
■ Give it away to someone in your family, to a friend, or to a neighbor. It's surprising to discover how much value others place on our castoffs. For example, your old costume jewelry might be a real treasure to a child. Religious and charitable organizations take donations, especially clean clothing. And don't overlook theater groups—most will welcome materials that can be used as props and costumes.

5. Putting It Away

Now you're ready to decide what is the right storage place for the things you want to store. As you consider the three aspects of putting things away, keep in mind the importance of good access.

What Kind of Space Is It?

Obviously, small toy pieces don't store well in a wide-mesh basket, and wet bath sponges shouldn't be put in a closed drawer. You might be able to take advantage of otherwise wasted space on high shelves by storing large items, such as serving pieces, there. This also frees the most accessible space for the things you use most frequently. It's difficult to reach much beyond the first row of an assortment of small items, such as cups and bowls, if you store them on the higher shelves. Try to match the type of storage space to the sizes and shapes of the items you'd like to store. If the type of space you have available doesn't meet your needs, see Chapters 3 and 4 to help you custom-tailor it.

Who Uses It?

People come in a variety of sizes and shapes. Children, for instance, are shorter than adults. Storage for them needs to be low—clothes-closet rods hung at child's-eye level—and compartmentalized to help them develop organizational skills. A toy chest, then, will work best if its large interior space is divided by a horizontal tray, or if it holds boxes that in turn house small toy parts. Grown-ups may need the same help if organization doesn't come easily to them. Look at page 7 to orient your storage plans to eye level and reach.

How Frequently Is It Used?

Categorize things by your need to get at them.

■ Very often. Give an item easy access by putting it in front or on top. Consider hooks on door backs, small drawers or drawer dividers, and eye-level shelves to keep frequently used items visible and close at hand.

■ Often. It can be behind, above, or below the frequently used items. Consider the back of an easy-access drawer, the shelf just above the closet rod, or middle shelves in an upper cupboard.

■ Not very often. The backs of bottom drawers or deep shelves; high shelves; low shelves; under the bed and at the back of the closet— put infrequently used things in these less-accessible spaces.

■ Almost never. This is dead storage—tax records, old school yearbooks, and family portraits. Before you consign anything to dead storage, give it a hard-eyed look: are you sure you want to keep it? If so, then off with it to the attic, the basement, the garage—places it takes an effort to reach.

What Makes Good Access?

■ Can you see it? Visual access is important. Memory plays tricks on us; we often forget what we own when we can't see it. Thus, tucking a set of soufflé dishes under the brushed-steel cake cover may be bad storage.

■ Can you reach it? Not everything has to be right at your fingertips, but put the things you use most often in the easiest-to-reach places.

■ Can you get it out? The closer you pack things together or the higher you stack them, the harder they are to use. Packing and stacking also tend to produce breakage; it's very easy to nudge a glass or a toy off a crowded shelf.

Structure and Style

A Word on Style

The process you have just completed—analyzing an area and conforming your storage to its characteristics and to the activities being carried out there—is a means of developing structure. You now know what goes where, and you either have or have planned to acquire the storage facilities you need, whether they be well-organized closets and drawers, new shelves, or a wall of cabinets. You know how your redesigned area works. But how does it look? That's a question of style.

Style individualizes structure, gives the bare bones of shelving and cabinetry a dress to wear. You'll want any additions to your home to harmonize with what's already there and to reflect your personal style. The overall effect will be most pleasing if you give some thought to just what your personal style is and design any changes to be consistent with it. In dealing with storage, you'll have such choices as:

■ open or covered shelving. Some people like the cozy workshop look of a room with things clustered on open shelves; others are not tidy enough to keep open shelves looking nice. Open shelving also invites dust and grease to settle on the stored items, so its owner should be a vigilant cleaner.

Style Punctuates Structure

In the open-shelf kitchen, what you store, you see. The look of your wares and equipment and your arrangement of them determine the visual effect. The uncomplicated structure forms the backdrop for a colorful someone-really-lives-here environment.

In the traditional kitchen, the cabinet faces are the most prominent feature. Because you conceal the things you store, how they look is not so important. Behind the doors is a wealth of storage components incorporating a variety of shelf and drawer designs.

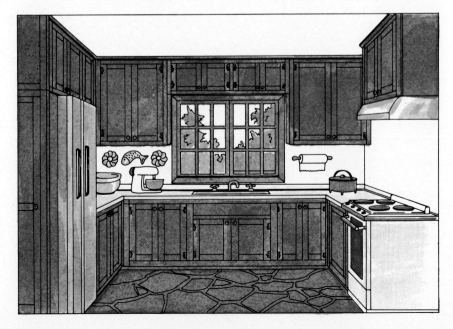

■ cabinet fronts. In kitchens, especially, and on cupboards and other pieces of wood furniture, style is strongly expressed by the kind of detailing on the doors. Consider a door with an inset molding-trimmed panel and an untrimmed door set flush to the cabinet frame—quite apart from the amount of dusting they require, they differ stongly in the style they create.

■ color scheme. A very simple room can handle an elaborate pattern or a multihued color scheme, but if you're cleverly maneuvering a large number of objects into a small space, or if you incline to keeping your belongings out where you can see them, your room probably has enough visual variety in it already. You'd be well advised to choose a quiet palette, perhaps even a monochromatic color scheme.

The four kitchens shown on these pages illustrate some style choices. What you see at first glance are the obvious differences: functional, open shelves; a cozy, traditional look; sleek contemporary lines; a no-nonsense work place. While each makes a completely different impression, you're not fooled. A kitchen is still a kitchen, no matter how it looks. All of them have the same storage spaces that kitchens normally provide—essentially, different forms of drawers and shelves. These components form your kitchen's structure, and they carry out their functions regardless of their style.

In the contemporary kitchen, ''less is more.'' All you see are clean, simple lines. Crisp, square edges and continuous flush fronts are the details of its style. All equipment is tucked away in cabinets fitted out with rollouts, lazy Susans, swing-out shelves—everything is at your fingertips.

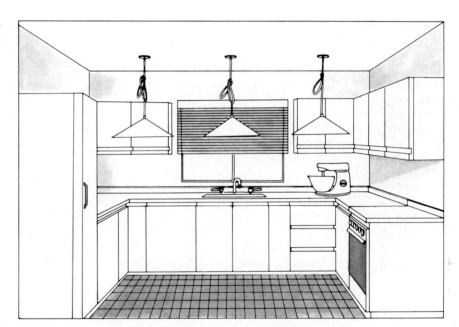

In the high-tech kitchen, convenience is king. Surfaces and materials are chosen for their function rather than their decorative effect. The tools and equipment *are* the style. See it, reach it, use it, clean it, and put it away. That's instant access, pure and simple.

Learn to look first for the type of storage space you need; recognize storage components by the jobs they do. Structure underlies style every time. Once you know what you're after functionally, you can add the ingredient of style, whether you build it or buy it.

A Potpourri of Project Ideas

This section shows ways you might put typical unused or underutilized spaces to work. To give you a clear picture of the different components that make up each storage scheme, the illustrations minimize style, concentrating only on the basic structure. Look at each scheme from two perspectives: the space it puts to work, and the combination of components employed. Use these project ideas as a springboard to get you started on a design of your own. Chapter 4 shows you how to plan, adapt, and build components for your particular situations.

Front Cover Closet

Here is a common situation in which a small closet has to do more than its fair share of work. The six-track system (page 63), a vertical module (page 69), and a self-supporting shelf (page 61) work together to yield a flexible, versatile closet system. Add purchased door-back hooks and wire pockets and slide-out wire baskets in stacking frames for a well-organized, compact storage system.

Shoe Rails

Shoes can be efficiently shelved on free-standing shoe rails of one, two, or even more levels. Use 3/4-inch plywood or particle board for the unit, and nail lengths of half-round molding to each shelf to hold the shoes in place. See self-supporting shelves (page 61) for the basic construction approach.

Entry-Hall Storage Wall

As traffic moves in and out a front door, the entryway often collects a cache of things-in-transit. Here, three plywood cases (two upright cases supporting a third that spans the width of the entryway) with doors and face frames fit together around the doorway to organize and store such items. The cupboard below the mail compartment and the mirrored cupboard above it contain shelving. See pages 75, 76, and 90 for component instructions.

A Potpourri of Project Ideas

Kitchen Base Cabinetry

Existing base cabinetry can yield a lot more storage capacity with just a few simple conversions. A heavy-duty rollout chopping block (page 71) slides in above the doors covering a bank of rollouts (page 72) and a set of vertical dividers (page 66). Drawer dividers (page 67) help organize the platform space in one rollout. All together, you can have at least five storage areas in the space of two shelves.

Appliance Garage

It's hard to use countertop work space when it's cluttered. Consider parking appliances like food processors, blenders, toasters, and other plug-in equipment in an appliance garage. Tri-folding doors mount to existing cabinetry and walls.

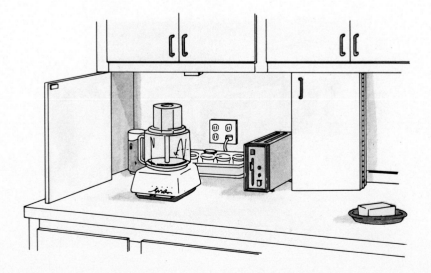

Box Drawers

Any unenclosed horizontal surface is a good candidate for a set of box drawers. A small-scale module (page 68) creates the pockets into which you slide simple butt-joint boxes or drawers (page 89) built to fit. Add hardware pulls or knobs, or cut curved pulls into the fronts.

Under-Sink Rollout

In the kitchen or bathroom, under-the-sink space is often wasted. Try this easy conversion: build a lipped rollout platform (page 72) to fit the cabinet. Then build a self-supporting shelf (page 61) just wide enough to fit inside the rollout's perimeter lip, and low enough to clear the plumbing. Screw the shelf to the platform and you have a double rollout.

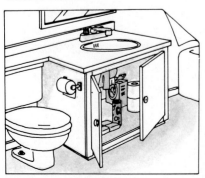

A Potpourri of Project Ideas

Garage Storage Units

Garages, carports, and other outside-the-house spots often need storage shelves and racks. Here are two cases made of 2 by 4 lumber frames, sheathed on the back and sides with 3/4-inch plywood. Separate them by a space equal to their own width. Build two frame-and-plywood doors and mount on heavy-duty sliding door track the length of the construction. The gap between the cases is a doorless storage space across which the doors slide to permit access to the cases' interior space.

Hammock Storage

Space over the hood of a car is generally wasted, yet it needn't be. Sling a net hammock there, and pitch all manner of odd-shaped, bulky things into it. Almost anything that isn't small, thin, or sharp can be stored in this fashion.

Storage Wall

Consider a back entry or porch as a place to keep rough-and-tumble things used outdoors but stored in the house. An assembly of plywood cases (page 75) join together to fill a small end wall with accessible storage space that includes deep rollouts (page 72), a fold-down door seat (page 76), and a six-track closet system (page 63).

A Potpourri of Project Ideas

Spare-Closet Workroom

Open this standard closet and you've got a whole workroom. Continuous hinge mounts a foldout work surface fastened to a vertical rollout (page 73) on casters. A second, unattached case (page 75) rolls out on casters to support the work surface mid-span. Shelves hang on track (page 63) in the closet, and the swing-out case of shelves holds accessories.

Concealed-Support Lumber Shelves

These shelves are sleek because the supports are concealed, and they are sturdy since they are made of 2-inch lumber. Steel dowel penetrates studs or masonry walls about 2-1/2 inches (see page 79 for marking and drilling) and slips into corresponding holes drilled in the lumber shelves to a depth of about 8 inches.

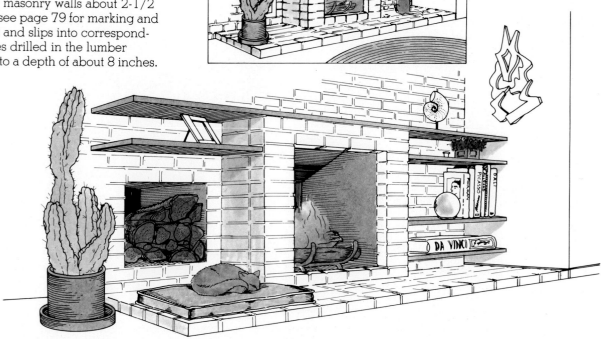

Chest-of-Drawers Bed

Why waste living space on bureaus for clothing when you can design and build a low "chest of drawers" that doubles as a bed frame platform? See pages 72 and 89 for rollout and drawer construction, and see cases and chests (pages 74–77) for the frame construction.

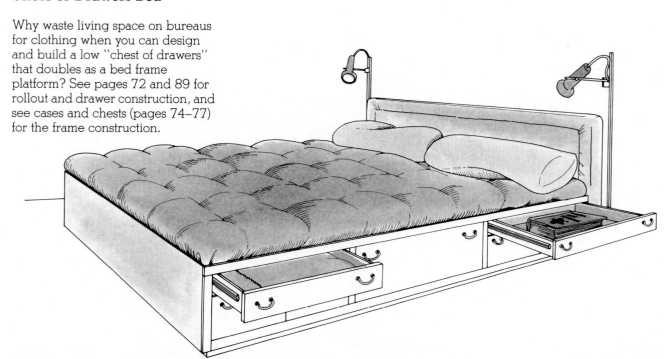

A Potpourri of Project Ideas

Kitchen Corner

With a scheme like this, you can design a delightful spot to relax and work in, and create a great deal of extra storage space too. See cleated shelves (page 62) for shelf mountings like those at the left, and cases and chests (pages 74–77) and rollouts (page 72) for the window seat with drawers and the case below the shelves.

Work Space in a Nook

Remove the shelves from a wall inset, and build a plywood case (page 75) sized to slip easily into the opening. Cover the joint of the case and wall with trim, and fit the case out with drawers (page 89), a fold-down writing desk (page 76), and shelves with covering doors.

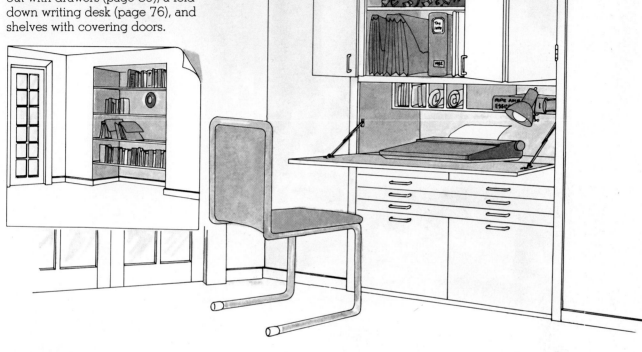

Door-Back Rack

Linens stay fresh and uncreased when you hang them on a lift-up door-back frame. See drilling (page 86) and butt joints (page 84) for the construction of the frame, and mount continuous hinge as in the chest on page 77.

Instant Solutions: Storage Products You Can Buy

From wall hooks to wall systems, ready-made products are quick answers to storage problems. Use this photographic guide to sample some options.

Now you're ready to get specific about adding new storage capacity. Chapter 1 helped you seek out "found" space—places that are either unused or underused. Chapter 2 showed you how to develop a well-thought-out plan for your space, and helped you determine where, how much, and what type of added storage facilities you might need. This chapter helps you consider the options available in ready-made products you can buy.

The basic need in storage is a way to gather up, organize, and keep track of things: a container. That container might be a small-scale component—even a shelf—or a large-scale item like a freestanding piece of furniture. In this chapter you'll see some options—counter, cabinet, and drawer accessories; boxes and bins; hangers, hooks, and wall-mounted storage; door-back and closet interior products; free-standing furniture that stores. Ready-made products are designed to satisfy a wide range of storage needs. The applications shown in these photographs are not the only possibilities; you can put the products to the use that works best for you.

Before purchasing a storage component, think about the characteristics of the items you plan to store in it. What are

their sizes and shapes? Are they fragile, heavy, rigid, soft? Do they need to be separated from other things, or enclosed? Should they have good air circulation? Each item's particular characteristics will describe a set of storage requirements that will help you make your selection.

In addition to these specific needs, keep the following criteria in mind as you make your selection:

■ the component's functional design: Does it meet your needs in terms of its structure? Is it flat or enclosed space, solid or open-work, stationary or movable, heavy-duty or light-duty? Is it made of materials appropriate for the application you plan?
■ its performance design: How will it perform in use? Will shelves, baskets, and frames remain stable, will surfaces and materials hold up under stress?
■ its versatility: Can the same piece be used for a different purpose later if your storage needs change?
■ its durability: Is it easy to maintain? Or will you have to replace it if it gets dirty?
■ its line, style, and color: Will it complement and harmonize with your environment?
■ its cost: Is it either reasonably priced, or of sufficient quality and value to merit the investment?

Many of these criteria, of course, will also apply if you build the components that solve your storage problems. Whether you build or buy, the goal is to make sure that your storage improvement truly meets your needs.

These modular plastic cubes line up, stack up, stand alone or in pairs, support counters, fit into closets, stand by the reading chair, or slip under your feet as you relax there—all with clean-lined good style. Because they're free-standing and finished on all sides, you can change the arrangement as you wish. Shelves fit on small clips and can be set at a number of different levels.

Boxes and Bins

Wheeled drawer and bin units glide smoothly around with you as you travel from room to room. The unit at left below is part of an extensive system of modular frames and vinyl-covered wire-mesh baskets of various sizes. The frames can be fitted with wheels, as shown here, or can stand alone, as in the unit shown in the closet on the front cover. That means that you can design a configuration tailored to your particular needs. The baskets are ideal for holding bulky objects or flat ones; kitchen, cleaning, and plant equipment, fabrics, paper, and clothing are among the possibilities. Drawer liners, racks, and top surfaces can be added to the basic unit.

The white-plastic taboret at right in the photograph on the opposite page gives you open compartments, swivel-out shelves, and bins. Available from artists' supply stores, taborets come in both plastic and metal, in a number of styles, sizes, and colors. Although they are intended to hold brushes, paints, and other art equipment, they are equally good at housing many other things. Needlework supplies are shown in the photograph; a taboret could also be helpful at the side of a desk or in a workshop. This type of component might work well as a child's toy chest; putting away playthings is easy and fun when the storage chest follows you around and then goes easily back to its home base.

Stackable plastic baskets

can be a good alternative to drawers. They come in many different configurations; some even slide into roll-around frames. Wide fronts make it easy to get things out, and because they're plastic, they are simple to clean. Baskets like the ones shown in the photograph at left below can be stacked four or five high and still maintain their stability. The slatted ones have the advantage of allowing air to circulate, which makes them good for bathroom supplies, as shown here, or for such food staples as potatoes, onions, and fruits. They come in several colors and two basket heights. The closed-side baskets have sufficient ventilation for storing fresh fruits and vegetables and are also handy for items such as cleaning supplies, toys, and even spare lightbulbs. Another variation on the stacking-basket theme is shown in the girl's closet on page 17, where plastic crates hold stuffed animals.

Cardboard file boxes are

purchased in a flat format; a few minutes of assembly give you very sturdy, ready-to-put-to-work, inexpensive storage. The file system comes in several bright colors and includes a set of hanging file folders that move smoothly along plastic edge pieces. Hand holds in the sides make the boxes easy to move from place to place. They're attractive enough to sit under a table or desktop as a substitute for a filing cabinet, and sturdy enough to stack in a closet, out of the way, filled with tax and other personal records. They're also the perfect size for record albums. Files of any sort, such as the travel clippings shown here, disappear from view under the colorful tops.

Cabinet and Counter Organizers

Cabinet and drawer interiors often invite improvement. And there are many possibilities. For example, the divided wooden tray at the bottom of the photograph on the opposite page is made for cutlery. But clearly it can help organize art or desk supplies, and it's also just the right size to hold 35mm photographic slides. To its right, a pair of lazy Susans—one free-standing, one to be installed on a corner door—are good ways to better utilize the inside corner space in base cabinetry, or deep pantry or closet space. The drawer system in the middle of the photograph is both free-standing and stackable. You can also purchase ready-made rollouts like the wooden one shown. Rollout vinyl-covered wire-mesh shelves such as the two-tier unit and the lid rack shown at the top of the photograph are other options. Stacked on the wooden drawer are divided jewelry and lingerie trays that help organize delicate things without snagging or scratching them.

An under-shelf basket like the one at right above fits neatly under any 3/4-inch shelf or tabletop on springy brackets. This one is vinyl-covered wire mesh with a little lip; there are a number of other types. Put one anywhere to use wasted headspace or to create a drawer. Shown above it is a two-tier freestanding lazy Susan, which increases access to the shelf space.

Wall-hung organizers can also be mounted on a cabinet door back or inside a closet. A bag-and-wrap holder, a sink-equipment caddy, and a cleaning-equipment hanger are representative of products manufactured for specialized storage but adaptable to other uses. The bag holder, for example, might hold rolls and sheet packages of giftwrap.

Clear plastic makes good storage pieces because you can see the contents easily. In the photograph below, food-processor blades are cached in a totable container made expressly for them. On the left are two hair-dryer stows. One holds the expected hair-care equipment. The other could sit on a kitchen counter, keeping utensils close at hand. The cosmetic organizer at right has plenty of compartments to keep the various items separated; in front, an identical unit becomes a mending box.

Wall Space Storage

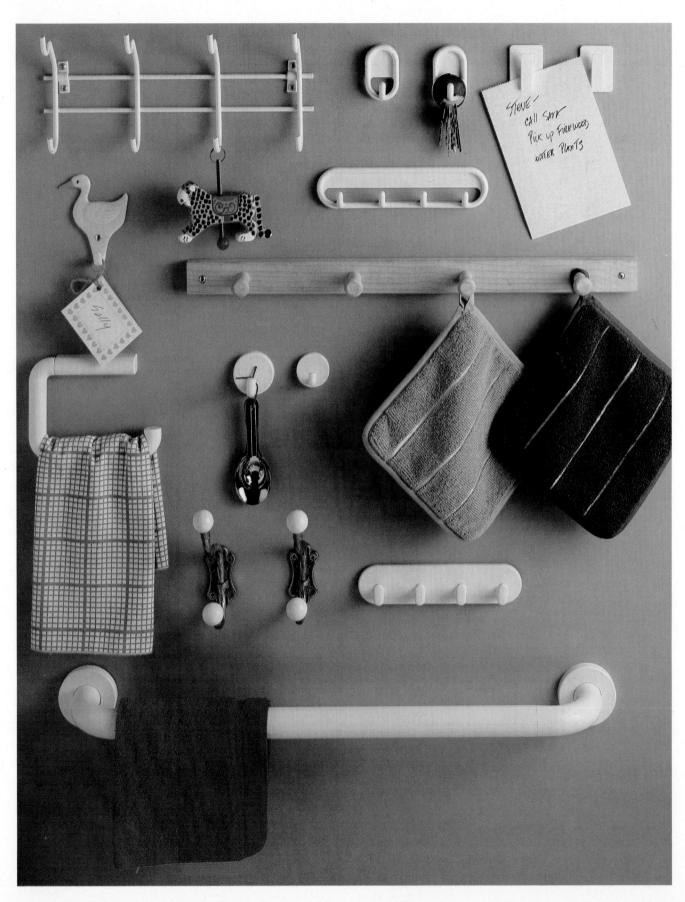

Hooks and hangers mount on many surfaces to improve the smooth functioning of your storage systems. These small accessories can play a major role in establishing style. You can choose from clean-lined plastic, practical vinyl-covered wire, warm-toned wood, old-fashioned ceramic, or whimsical animal designs. Most come in a number of colors as well. Select the type that harmonizes with and supports the style of your room. In closets, cupboards, and corners, on door backs and walls, hooks and hangers can quickly and inexpensively expand your storage capacity. But be wary of installing too many—they can add up to visual chaos. A few carefully selected wall mountings go a long way.

Iron, ironing board, sleeve board, light, and door-mounted hook make up a compact ironing center that's perfect for a small-space situation. Or this could be the way to put the ironing board where you use it—ready in an instant, easy to put away, and with all the necessary equipment right at hand. Sized to fit in standard wood-frame wall construction, the cabinet comes with all fittings installed. Its exterior and interior can be given a natural wood finish or painted; when closed, it looks like a wall cupboard.

The wall-mounted grid comes in a number of sizes and colors and can be used singly or in combination. Baskets of several proportions mount on movable hooks for a storage system that easily accommodates different sizes and shapes. The hooks themselves hold items anywhere on the grid. The system works well in almost any part of the house where visible storage is appropriate. In the kitchen, a grid will hang pots, pans, and utensils; mounted on a door back, it will improve a closet's storage capacity. The grids are particularly useful for basement, garage, or bathroom storage because their vinyl covering makes them rustproof.

Door Backs and Closet Interiors

Vinyl-covered wire shelving (left below) is sturdy, lightweight, easy to keep clean, and easy to install. The open-work construction means good ventilation for the contents, and, in addition to its practical virtues, the shelving has simple, clean-lined looks. This system consists of open-ended shelves, available in several lengths, and mounting brackets. You decide the intervals between shelves and the length your shelving will run.

The brackets can be quickly removed, so you can reposition the shelves as needed. Beneath the shelves in the photograph below are drawers made of clear plastic, so you can see what they contain. Interlocking frames let you stack them safely. Available in several sizes, they're useful storage components in many places, particularly on shelves with a lot of unused headspace.

Door backs contribute a significant amount of storage potential in any space. Systems of the type shown in the photograph below right help you use them to full advantage. It's simple to screw the verticals to the door back; adjustable vinyl-covered wire baskets, available in two widths sized to standard doors, fit easily into the verticals. A similar, lighter-duty unit with fixed shelves is shown on the door back of the closet on the front cover.

Canvas pouches make up a king-size shoe bag (below left). It will hold 12 pairs of shoes, a big help to many an overcrowded closet. But perhaps you'd rather mix its functions, as suggested by the photograph: think of your stereo headset; ballet slippers; hammer, screwdriver, pliers, and folding rule; mittens and caps; stockings, socks, and lingerie; scarves, belts, and clutch bags; maps. What about stuffed animals or toy trucks? The pouch unit can be hung on a door back or wall anywhere in the house that you need a storage helper.

A new closet interior can be purchased from a closet specialty shop. You'll be able to select from a variety of standard options, and the structure will be built to fit your particular closet space. This one features wall-mounted pole and shelf track, which makes the major horizontal elements fully adjustable. The vertical module contains shelves and drawers in a case. You can choose enough drawers to replace your dresser, if you wish, or fill the module with adjustable shelves instead. Or use the module to divide a wider closet, and hang a full-height clothes rod on the other side. Shown inside this closet: more stackable plastic drawers and baskets to hold socks and other small items of clothing. Don't forget the many kinds of hangers—individual or six-at-a-time skirt hangers, blouse or shirt hangers, special belt and tie holders—that can help you use closet space to best advantage.

Furniture That Stores

A reproduction armoire such as the one shown on the opposite page can be ordered with the inside configuration of shelves and drawers that best suits your needs. This one is intended for a bedroom, where it will add warmth and charm while storing clothing in its drawers and spare bedding and other items on its shelves. You can use baskets, as shown here, to hold small things—socks, perhaps. The piece is sized to accommodate the television as well—you can watch from bed, then close the doors when the TV is not in use. A piece such as this would also be at home in a living room or family room.

Ready-made wall systems

like the one shown at right are a simple, attractive way to organize your living space. Components include a bar unit; a desk; a sliding television platform; and drawers, shelves, and vertical compartments in a number of sizes. You specify the arrangement that will work best for you. In small living spaces, this kind of concentrated storage can give you the efficient, well-ordered look you want. Even where space is less of a problem, a wall system can bring order to a jumble of worldly goods, turning a liability into a room-enhancing asset.

This rosewood home office (at bottom) hides its secret well. Closed, it's simply an attractive wood cabinet that could hold a row of books along the back half of its top. But open, it reveals a compact, well-organized work space that contains just about everything a home office might require. On the wings, shelves hold paper and other supplies above

compartments fitted to hold file folders. The fold-down work surface is securely supported on the wings; in the back are more compartments and an extendable lamp that's part of the unit. Below, large books and even a decorative pot find room. Full-depth feet stabilize the piece and continuous piano hinge ensures its strength.

Tailor-Made Solutions: Storage Components You Can Build

Storage schemes are made of basic components: shelves, pockets, dividers, modules, rollouts, cases, chests, and racks. This chapter shows you how to design and construct your own. A special illustrated section helps you with Tools, Techniques, and Tips.

This chapter shows you how to build the basic components of storage. Each represents a part of any storage project. No dimensions are included for any component; that permits you to tailor the size to your own particular space situation. When you master the layout, design, and construction method, you can freely adapt the concept as needed. Once you can build single components, you'll be able to apply the same skills to make any combination you choose to construct. Thus the instructions here are the key to storage improvements ranging from a single drawer or shelf to a whole houseful of projects.

The components are arranged in a skill-building order. The first ones are the simplest; the construction methods needed are basic. Succeeding projects graduate in the levels of skill and experience you'll need. You can plunge in at any point; if you are new to woodworking and are not familiar with the process of construction, you may want to read the section on tools, techniques, and tips (pages 80–93) before you proceed. It is organized in the order of the steps commonly used on any building project.

The instructions in this chapter show you how to tailor-make the components to the dimensions of your living space. You can add shelf capacity with self-supporting shelves, install cleats to support shelves, or mount track to walls or other vertical surfaces for adjustable shelving. Pockets will allow you to convert any door back into drawer space. Vertical dividers form ideal storage spaces for thin, flat items; horizontal dividers do the same job of concentrating the use you get out of storage volume. See the closet on the front cover for an example of what modules can do for you: the large-scale vertical module holds a set of adjustable shelves. A large-scale horizontal module could be mounted across the top; see page 60 for an illustration of these components used together. Modules at a smaller scale hang from the bottom of any horizontal surface. Rollouts can be built in any size or shape that your imagination conceives, and installed in any configuration you choose.

All the above components are excellent for making conversions to your existing storage space. Cases and chests bring you to furniture-scale projects. They offer a variety of styles as well as storage capacity. Racks, too, yield generous storage space and are excellent components where visual effect is not of great importance. Like cases and chests, they excel at adding storage where none already exists. They are easy to build, relatively inexpensive, and need no particular finish treatment.

Keep in mind that woodworking is a personal craft. Although the techniques are tried and true, the way you'll do each task will depend on your individual experience, rhythm, and tools. You'll do your building in the way that is most comfortable for you. Even if your workshop consists of a closet where you keep a few tools, many of the projects are within your reach. Whatever your level of skill, among these components may be the answer to your storage problems.

This plywood chest (instructions on page 77) is made with simple butt joints and rests on a separate pedestal with a curved-cut foot (see page 76). Stock cove molding is attached to the top and front to make a pull for the lift-up lid. Designed as a dressing bench that will hold clothing or blankets at the foot of a bed, the chest is a comfortable height for sitting, which means it also makes a pleasant window seat, as shown here.

Adding Shelf Capacity

Whether you need more capacity in an existing shelf system or you want to create shelves in a new place, the components described below can help. Each of these three basic types—self-supporting shelves, cleated shelves, and the six-track system—meets storage needs in a different way. Full- or partial-depth self-supporting shelves are the easiest and least expensive to build; cleated shelves are handsome and particularly strong; and the six-track system affords great versatility and flexibility.

Any of these three shelf types is a good project for a beginner, since they require only basic woodworking tools and techniques. Building any of these units will get you warmed up for other component projects and, for a modest investment of time and money, will produce good, quick solutions to some of your most pressing storage problems.

How do you choose which type of shelf to use? Think about where you plan to put the shelving, what you want it to look like, how you want it to work, and what tools and skills you have. Consult the illustrations and descriptions below to decide which type of component will add the shelf capacity you need.

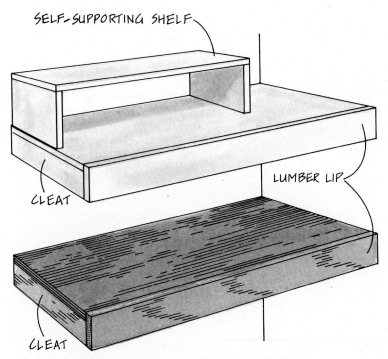

SELF-SUPPORTING SHELF

LUMBER LIP

CLEAT

CLEAT

CLEATED SHELVES

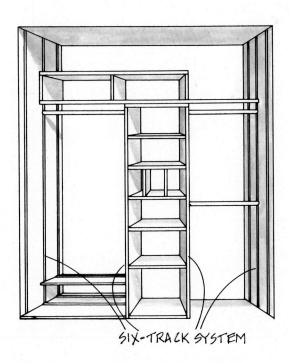

SIX-TRACK SYSTEM

Self-Supporting Shelves. On any exposed surface, or where existing shelves are too far apart so that the space between them is wasted, adding self-supporting shelves will increase your storage capacity. Build them in the height, width, and depth that reflect the items you plan to store on them.

To install one of these shelves, you simply set it in place. Because they aren't fastened down, no surface repair is needed when you relocate them, which makes them particularly useful if you rent your dwelling. As your storage patterns change, you can rearrange these components according to your new needs.

Cleated Shelves. You can mount cleated shelves in any space with two parallel or adjacent vertical surfaces, such as an opening between a wall and the side of a cabinet, in a closet, under stairs, or in a nook. Cleated shelves are sturdy, stable, and capable of bridging fairly long spans, especially when they are supported on three sides.

Since cleated shelves are not adjustable, it's best to use them where you want shelves to become part of the architecture. The cleats are fastened directly to wall surfaces, so measure carefully when you position them; mistakes will require surface repairs.

Six-Track System. People's clothing storage patterns change: young people grow, fashions shift, wardrobes expand and contract. Some people, such as the very tall, the very short, and the handicapped, need specially designed closets. With the six-track system you can arrange your closet to give you easy access to every cubic foot of storage space. Let your wardrobe and your imagination guide you as you plan pole heights and design components that meet your present storage needs. If your living and storage patterns change, the six-track system allows you to rearrange your closet interior.

Self-Supporting Shelves

You can build self-supporting shelves quickly and easily using simple butt joints and common materials; or you can make a handsome version with a finer hardwood and miter joints.

Place self-supporting shelves on exposed surfaces to create mini shelf units, or set them at the back of enclosed spaces to store small items that otherwise get lost among larger things. You can improve the effectiveness of storage space in kitchen cabinets, bathroom vanities, linen, utility and front hall closets (such as the one shown on the cover) by adding self-supporting shelves.

Construction. Measure the space and record the dimensions on a freehand sketch. Take particular care with inside measurements, and be sure to account for the barrel of the tape.

When you plan the component's dimensions, remember that face frames and closet side-wall overhangs can restrict your ability to move a full-length shelf into place. Unless there is plenty of space between existing shelves, build the component shorter than the full interior width.

Cut your materials to size; apply 1/4-inch by 3/4-inch lumber strips or veneer tape to unfinished plywood edges if you wish. If you're using softwood lumber or plywood, assembly will be easier if you start the nails in the top. If you're using particle board or hardwood lumber, predrill for screws, using a countersink bit.

Apply a thin layer of white glue to the end-grain of one side piece. Lay the top over the glued side piece, hold it flush and square, and fasten it down. (Rest the unglued side piece under the top to support it during this process.) Then glue and fasten the other side piece to the top. Set and putty the nail heads, or glue and plug the screw heads.

Let the assembly dry, then sand and finish it. You're ready to set the shelf in place and use it.

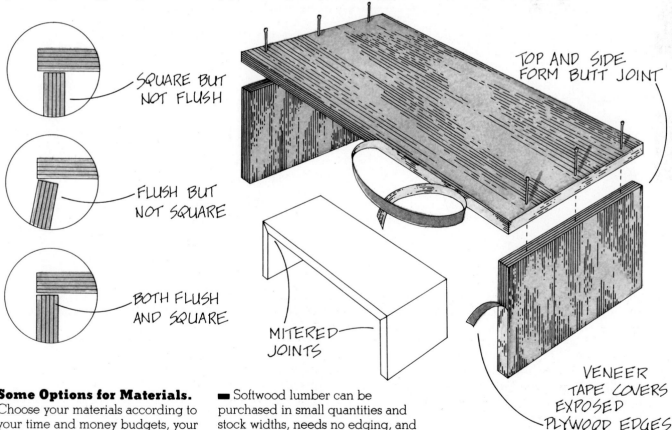

SQUARE BUT NOT FLUSH

FLUSH BUT NOT SQUARE

BOTH FLUSH AND SQUARE

TOP AND SIDE FORM BUTT JOINT

MITERED JOINTS

VENEER TAPE COVERS EXPOSED PLYWOOD EDGES

Some Options for Materials.

Choose your materials according to your time and money budgets, your skills, your tools, and the finished look you want to achieve.

■ Particle board is inexpensive and comes in stock widths; all you have to do is cut the pieces to length. Plan to predrill and screw the parts together.

■ Softwood lumber can be purchased in small quantities and stock widths, needs no edging, and can be nailed without predrilling.
■ Hardwood lumber has the same merits as softwood, except that it needs to be predrilled and screwed. Like softwood, hardwood lends itself to fine joinery; plugged screw heads at a butt joint can add a very nice touch.

■ Plywood needs to be ripped to width and cut to length, and if you want to cover the exposed plies, it needs to be edged. These processes aren't difficult, but they do require extra work.

Adding Shelf Capacity

Cleated Shelves

Two parallel upright surfaces are the key to these easily installed, good-looking shelves. Cleat-mounting has been used for centuries. Cleated shelves can bear a lot of weight, and you can take advantage of this fact by storing heavy things—television, stereo components, records, or books—on them. You can also use cleats to build a sturdy, ample working shelf: in the kitchen, cleat-mount a slab of chopping block; in the bedroom or the study, mount a hollow-core door.

Some Options on Design. Different construction materials give you a number of options for cleated-shelf design.

■ For shelves, use edged 3/4-inch plywood or hardwood or softwood lumber of any thickness, or consider mounting 1/4-inch plate glass on large quarter-round cleats.
■ For concealed cleating, you might use ripped plywood or particle-board strips. Conceal the cleating by attaching a lumber 1 by 3 lip to the front of each shelf.

■ If you wish the cleating to show, use an attractive stock molding, 1-inch quarter-round, 1 by 2 lumber, or any other material with at least one flat side. For a three-sided support, miter the joints of the back and side cleats. To expose the cleating, don't put a lip on the shelf.
■ Paint the shelves the wall color to blend them into their environment, or apply a natural wood finish for contrast.

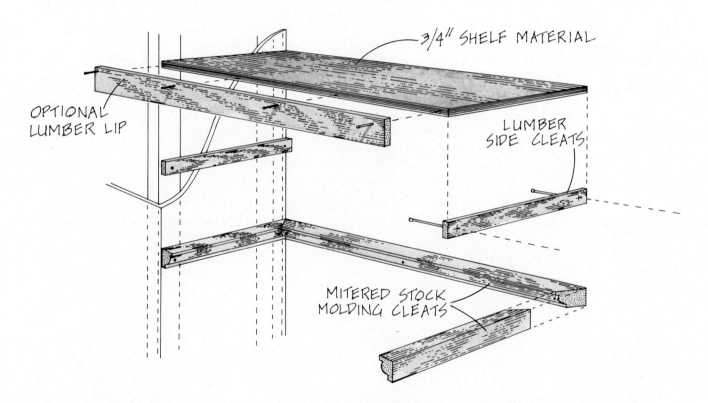

OPTIONAL LUMBER LIP

3/4" SHELF MATERIAL

LUMBER SIDE CLEATS

MITERED STOCK MOLDING CLEATS

Construction. Measure the space and record your dimensions on a freehand sketch.

Cut your cleating material to length. If you're using two cleats, they can be the full depth of the shelf, or 1/4 inch to 1/2 inch less. For butt-joined cleating on three sides, make the back cleat flush to each side wall, then butt the side cleats to it. For mitered cleating, each cleat's wall face will be full length.

When you cleat the inside of a

cabinet, you should use only side cleats. Cabinet backs are often surface-nailed 1/4-inch material. Nailing a back cleat to such a back may well knock it off.

If you can locate the studs, mount the cleating to them with nails or screws. If you can't find the studs, mount the cleats with hollow-wall fasteners. If the wall is brick, concrete, or tile, drill it with a masonry bit. Then drill corresponding holes in the cleats and fasten them to the wall using

expansion shields and screws.

Cut the shelf material to size, allowing about 1/8 inch clearance to slip the shelf into place. Edge the shelf, and putty and sand it as needed. Apply natural wood finishes now; if you're painting, wait until shelves are in place.

Place the shelves on the cleats. If you'd like to attach them permanently, predrill, and then nail through the shelf surface into the top edge of the cleat. Set the nails and putty the holes.

Six-Track System

The amount of capacity the six-track system generates in an average closet borders on the miraculous. Most closets are under-equipped; the usual fixed shelf over an adult-height closet pole provides only limited wardrobe storage. Tremendous wasted space glares out from under shirts and skirts hung on full-width poles.

With this kind of arrangement, it's not easy to create the versatile and flexible closet you'd like. With a six-track system, though, you can tailor a closet for any member of the household at a small investment of both time and money. You need not confine this system to closets; mount it between any two parallel walls for excellent storage space.

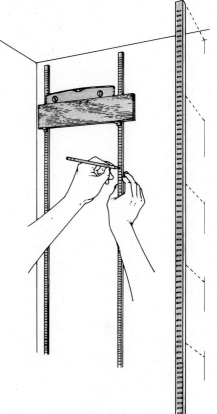

LEVELING
THE TRACKS

Design and Construction.

Measure your closet space and record the dimensions on a freehand sketch. Make a note of anything that will bear on your design: the door opening, the way the door is mounted (hinges, bifolding pivots, sliding-door track), closet side-wall overhangs, interior baseboard, and existing closet fittings.

Plan your closet layout. If your closet has a door opening between 30 inches and 48 inches wide and an interior up to 60 inches wide, plan to mount three shelf tracks on each side wall. For wider closets, add a divider (see below) or a vertical module (see pages 68–69); then double the six-track system, so that each pair of vertical surfaces has a set of six tracks. The doubled six-track system will allow more versatility in the use of space, and will give better weight-bearing capacity by allowing you to use shorter-span shelves and poles.

If your design doesn't include using existing closet fittings in their present positions, remove them now. On one side wall only, mark the positions of the tracks; place the middle track about 11 inches from the back wall. Clothes rods will hang

from this track; half-depth shelves and modules will hang from the middle track and the back one; full-depth components will hang from all three tracks.

Position the first track, and check to see that it's plumb. Through one screw-hole, drill a pilot hole, and then loosely drive the screw in. Recheck the track to be sure it is plumb, and drill the other screw-holes; then screw the track down securely. To assure that the clip slots are level with one another, insert a clip in a numbered slot on the fastened track; insert another clip in the next track's corresponding slot. Hold the second track in its approximate position and rest a piece of flat scrap across both clips. Place a level on the scrap, and adjust the second track until the bubble is centered, and pencil-mark several screw locations. (You may find this process easier with a helper.) Drill and screw this track down like the first; repeat this process for the remaining tracks.

When all the tracks are installed, measure the width of the space between the track's faces. Then cut the shelves and poles to size, allowing clearance as needed.

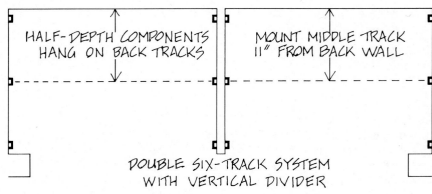

HALF-DEPTH COMPONENTS HANG ON BACK TRACKS

MOUNT MIDDLE TRACK 11" FROM BACK WALL

DOUBLE SIX-TRACK SYSTEM
WITH VERTICAL DIVIDER

Closet Divider. First, before installing any track, cut the divider to size, or construct a module. Then, on each outside face of the divider or module, mount three tracks as described above. Cleat or toenail the divider into place; screw or nail

the module to the floor and back wall.

Now install three tracks on each remaining closet side wall according to the instructions given above. Take care to match the slots so that your shelves and poles will be level.

Pockets

Consider the door back: First, it's a good mounting surface; second, it's easy to get to; and third, it's already attached to your closets and cabinetry. Add these merits up and you discover a hidden storage potential. Door-back pockets transform this potential into efficient storage space and put frequently used things conveniently at your fingertips; just open the door for instant access. You will also notice that drawers, cabinets, and closets work much more efficiently when you've lightened their storage load by putting some of their contents into door-back pockets.

Use pockets to turn your closet into a one-stop dressing room. Stockings, socks, underwear, lingerie, accessories, combs, and brushes all slip into pockets with ease, freeing drawer space and putting your whole wardrobe in one

place. If you've got bi-folding or sliding doors, replace them with hinged doors to take advantage of pockets.

Pockets also solve bathroom storage problems easily and well. Design them to hold grooming or shaving things—hair equipment such as dryers, curlers, and combs; makeup, lotions, sundries, and soaps; facecloths, sponges, and the children's bath toys.

In the kitchen, mount pockets on cabinet door backs. Small containers such as yeast packets, condiments and spices, or heavy cans, bottles, and jars store equally well here. Slip lids into pockets that are fitted with lengthwise dividers; you'll free cabinet space, and the lids will be easy to take out and replace. See pages 66 and 67 for information on dividers.

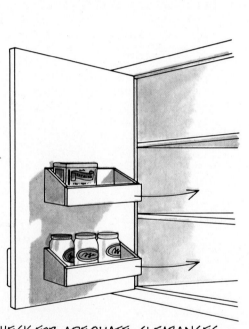

CHECK FOR ADEQUATE CLEARANCES.
CHECK FOR INSET AND VERTICAL ALIGNMENT.

BACKING SHEET

Designing Pockets. Each pocket consists of sides, bottom, a front or lip, and a back, plus any interior partitions you might add. As you plan your pockets, keep in mind:

■ the number and size of the items you plan to store there. This will guide you in figuring the height and depth of the pocket and the shape of the lip.
■ clearance for closing the door. The door swings in an arc; the pocket must be inset enough to allow the door to close.
■ the pocket's vertical alignment. You don't want it bumping into either the existing shelves or their contents.

■ the door material and construction. Solid doors can receive the pockets directly. Older cabinet doors are almost always made of solid material, which is a good mounting surface. New cabinet doors may be hollow-core, panel-frame, or metal, and will need a 1/2-inch backing sheet. To determine your door's material and construction, tap gently across the face of it; if it sounds tinny or hollow, it probably is.

Measure the space, noting existing shelves and other factors (door knobs, backing plates, hinge positions) that may affect your plan. Record the dimensions on a freehand sketch. Plan the number of

X IS EQUAL TO OR GREATER THAN Y

pockets you want, their sizes and shapes, and their positions on the door. Use the sketch to figure the length-to-depth ratio so that your door can still close. The formula is this: The pocket must be inset from the door's opening edge by an amount equal to or greater than the length of the side.

Construction. Cut the material to size; if you want curved front lips, make these cuts now, using a curve-cutting saw.

Assemble the parts with glue and nails or with screws. First fasten the sides to the bottom, then apply the front and back, and insert and fasten any interior dividers. If you are applying the pockets directly to a solid door, sand and finish them as desired.

Hold the pocket in place on the door back and check to be sure the door will close. If there's a problem, reposition the pocket closer to the hinge side so that the door will still open and close. Predrill for the screws and fasten the pocket onto the door back. For panel-frame, hollow-core, or sheet-metal doors, use the backing sheet method.

Backing Sheet Method.
Measure the surface to which you will mount pockets; note factors such as door stops, door knobs, and backing plates that will prevent a snug fit between the door back and the backing sheet. Record the dimensions on your sketch, and plan a backing sheet of 1/2-inch plywood large enough to overlap the solid perimeter, yet small enough to miss the obstructions; cut a notch in the backing sheet to fit around the door knob and plate if you need to. (To determine the dimensions of the solid perimeter, tap across the door face, listening for the spot at which the hollow sound stops.) Check your measurements again and cut the backing sheet to size. Mark the positions of the pockets directly on the backing sheet. Measure again to be sure the door will close, and then screw the pockets down.

Hold the backing sheet and pocket assembly in place on the door back and check again to be sure the door will close. Mark the position of the assembly, and predrill the screw-holes. Then mount the assembly, using wood screws for wood doors or sheet-metal screws for sheet-metal doors. Paint, or finish with stain and a sealer coat.

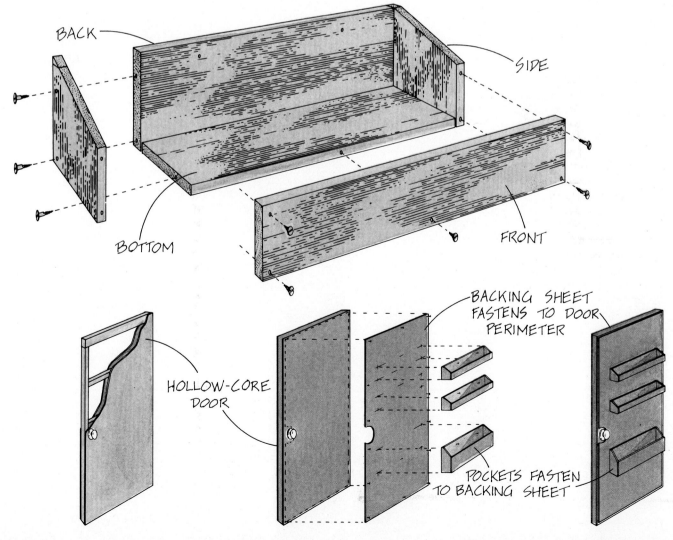

Dividers

Dividing your existing storage space can multiply its capacity. Dividers tailor the shape of the volume to the shape of what you store there. Both vertical and horizontal dividers are simple to build. They visually organize and sort the things you store—and what you can see, you'll be more likely to use.

Vertical Dividers

Vertical dividers support thin, rigid things on edge—baking tins, platters and trays, sewing patterns, records, art supplies. Slip articles such as these between 1/4-inch hardboard, plywood, or plexiglass dividers to make a convenient, concentrated storage space. But you need not stop with small items: card tables, folding chairs, trays, table leaves, and even supplies of plywood are safely and accessibly stored between sturdy 1/2-inch or 3/4-inch vertical dividers.

Construction. Measure the enclosed space and record the dimensions on a freehand sketch. If the space doesn't have a continuous upper surface to which you can fasten spacers, install one: cleat the perimeter of the enclosure so that the bottoms of the cleats are 1 inch above the cabinet opening and nail a piece of 3/4-inch plywood to the bottom of the cleats. Adjust the height recorded on your sketch accordingly.

Based on what you plan to store in each compartment, determine the number of dividers you'll install. Then cut them to size, subtracting 1/16 inch from the height for clearance. For easy access, you might want a curved cut on the front edges; if so, use a coping, saber, or band saw. Sand smooth and finish.

Cut a pair of 1/4-inch plywood spacers for each compartment; spacer width will determine compartment width, so size them to what you plan to store. To install, start at one side of the enclosure. Nail the first pair of spacers to the top and bottom of the enclosure, butting the edges flush against the side wall. Set a vertical divider in place, and nail down the next pair of spacers so that they are flush against it. Continue to the other side, and end with a pair of spacers.

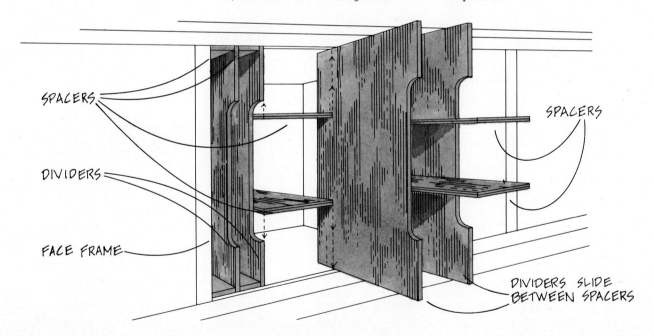

SPACERS

DIVIDERS

FACE FRAME

SPACERS

DIVIDERS SLIDE BETWEEN SPACERS

Variations. Vertical dividers are most often installed in base and wall-hung cabinets and in closet space between fixed horizontal surfaces. But adjustable shelves can house dividers just as well. To install them, measure the height between two shelves—this, less 1/16 inch allowance for clearance, will be the height to which you will cut the dividers. Then remove the shelves, place them edge to edge, and mark the divider placements across the face of both with a pencil and a square. Cut the dividers and spacers to size. Working from one side of each shelf to the other, attach the spacers to the top of one shelf and the bottom of the other, using a divider to establish the gap between spacers. Remount the shelves and slide the dividers into place.

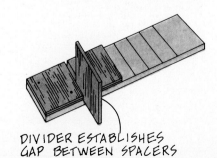

DIVIDER ESTABLISHES GAP BETWEEN SPACERS

Horizontal Dividers

Horizontal dividers are simply sliding trays, and you can store more on them than meets the eye. Why? Because pulling out the tray gives access to things at the back. You can get full use of your existing storage volume by mounting horizontal dividers close together; since they slide out, you get good access even with minimal headspace.

Construction. Measure the space and record the dimensions on a freehand sketch. Measure any face frame overhangs; you will shim out the sides of the enclosure so that the trays can slide out between the overhangs. Determine the distance between trays according to the height of what you plan to store there; you need to allow only minimal headspace. Mark the positions on the enclosure's sides. This is where you will position the shims and side cleats, so use a carpenter's level to make sure that the marks are level front to back and that each horizontal pair is positioned on the same level plane.

The diagrams below show three ways to make your slide cleats. You'll need two full-depth cleats for each tray. Make up your cleat stock in a convenient length—perhaps 8 feet—then cut the cleats to size.

At the tray position marks, shim out the sides of the enclosure enough that when the cleats are installed, the slide grooves will clear the face frame. Predrill and nail on the slide cleats, rechecking to be sure that the two cleats of each pair are level and parallel to one another.

To determine the tray dimensions, measure the interior depth of the enclosure behind the face frame. Then measure the operating width of the slide cleats, and subtract 1/16 inch for clearance. Cut the trays to size, and sand the exposed surfaces. Then glue and nail 1 by 1 strips on top along all four edges as shown. Sand, and finish with plastic sealer or a semigloss paint. Insert trays in the slide cleats. For smooth sliding, wax the tray tongues with paraffin.

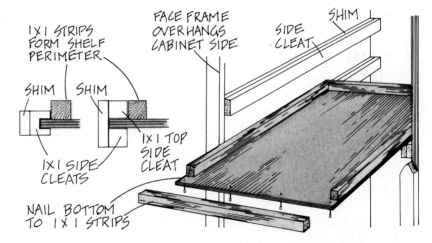

Drawer Dividers

Any drawer can house vertical dividers of full or partial depth. Deep drawers can be split into two levels as well: cleat the long side above the dividers and rest a tray on top.

Construction. Rip 1/4-inch or 1/2-inch lumber or plywood to the divider depth you choose. Cut pieces to length according to your design. You can use a mix of both 1/4-inch and 1/2-inch stock in the same drawer according to where you need the extra strength and where you want the extra space. The diagrams show some configurations.

■ Partial: nail or dado the back to dividers and insert in drawer. Tack 1/4-inch spacers to the drawer front, and side-nail the cross partition in place.

■ Cross: side-nail dividers in place, or tack 1/4-inch spacers to the drawer sides.
■ Lengthwise: tack spacers to drawer front and back, inserting dividers as you proceed from one side to the other.
■ Combinations: tack spacers to drawer sides after side-nailing the cross dividers.

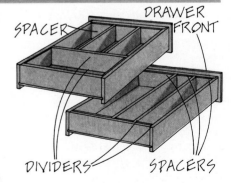

An Insert Tray. Plan the tray's height, then nail 1 by 1 cleats onto the drawer sides at a level that will allow the drawer to close. To build the tray, cut a 1/2-inch plywood bottom piece; glue and nail on edging made of 1/2-inch lumber (drawer stock); let the lumber sides cover the plywood edge. Set the tray into place on the side cleats.

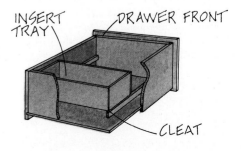

Modules

Modules are essentially upside-down self-supporting shelves. Hung from the bottom of kitchen cabinets, **small-scale modules** allow you to put supplies and light-weight equipment right above the work areas where you need them. Fold-down doors can cover the contents. Wire baskets for vegetables and fruits stored at room temperature can be slipped into open-faced modules, as can covered boxes for staples. Add a middle shelf to one section, and you can store spices there too. **Large-scale modules** do bigger jobs. Sweaters, shirts, shoes, bags, hats, and boots are some of the many things you can keep conveniently in closet modules.

Small-Scale Modules

Here are some possible configurations for small-scale modules. Use 3/4-inch softwood lumber or plywood. To achieve a unified look, finish your modules to match existing surfaces.

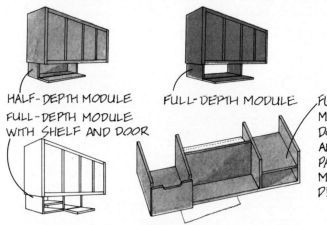

HALF-DEPTH MODULE

FULL-DEPTH MODULE WITH SHELF AND DOOR

FULL-DEPTH MODULE

FULL-DEPTH MODULE WITH DOOR, SHELF, AND DIVIDER; PAPER TOWELS MOUNT BEHIND DIVIDER

Under-Cabinet Module Construction. Measure the space for the module, including the depth of the recess formed by the cabinet sides and bottom shelf. Record all dimensions on a freehand sketch. Plan your cutting list, keeping in mind that:

■ the sides will extend into the recess under the cabinet and butt against the cabinet bottom; the sides will also overlay the module's bottom piece. Account for this extra length and cut the sides so that the finished opening is the size you want.
■ the bottom will butt between the sides.
■ upright dividers should be 3/4 inch shorter than the side pieces, since the dividers butt against the module's bottom piece.
■ the door should be cut shorter than the sides so that it closes under the face frame.
■ if you include a back, it will butt against the module's sides and bottom piece.

Cut your materials to size. If you're using plywood, determine which edges will be exposed and cover them with veneer tape. If you want a shaped edge for opening the door

instead of a hardware pull, cut it now, using a curve-cutting saw. Sand all surfaces. Mark the position of the angle-bracket screw-holes, predrill, and screw the angle brackets to the sides and dividers.

To assemble the module, start your nails in one side piece. Apply glue to the bottom and side piece where they will join, and nail them together. Repeat the process for the divider and the other side piece. Set the nail heads and putty the holes, then let the assembly dry.

Position the module in the cabinet recess and mark the angle-bracket screw-holes. Remove the module, and predrill. Finish both the unit and the door before you install them. When they are dry, screw a length of continuous hinge to the door and then screw that to the unit; you may need to predrill. Now install the unit under the cabinet. Then mount a spring or magnetic catch for the door, and a fold-down door stop if you want to limit the door's swing to 90 degrees.

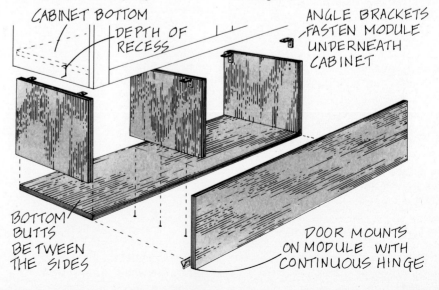

CABINET BOTTOM

DEPTH OF RECESS

ANGLE BRACKETS FASTEN MODULE UNDERNEATH CABINET

BOTTOM BUTTS BETWEEN THE SIDES

DOOR MOUNTS ON MODULE WITH CONTINUOUS HINGE

Large-Scale Modules

Large-scale modules can be built vertically for space-dividing storage units or horizontally for longer shelf surfaces. Large-scale modules are key components in the six-track closet system (see page 63).

Closets and Verticals. In closets with interior widths up to 60 inches and a single door opening, install a single piece of 3/4-inch plywood to divide the space vertically; a vertical module would use too much space.

In closets more than 60 inches wide, with door openings larger than 36 inches, vertical modules will work very well. One good basic design has a module in the center, built high enough that you can hang dresses and longer clothing on one side, and two rows of skirts, shirts, and pants on the other. A horizontal module can rest on top so that it has extra support over the longer span.

Horizontal Modules

- Modules mounted over eye-level closet poles will work best if you build them no deeper than 12 inches to 15 inches, so that you can see and reach the back.
- Modules or shelves mounted below eye-level will work best if you build them 20 inches to 22 inches deep: on the six-track system, all three tracks on each side will support them.
- Modules that run full-length from wall to wall must be designed with offset compartments to allow them to be moved into position. The offset should equal the height of the compartment.
- Modules that run between a wall and a vertical component don't need to be offset since you can install the horizontal module in the closet before you add the vertical component; once in position, the horizontal module can be adjusted up and down easily.

Construction. Measure your closet space—its overall height and depth, its working width (the distance between faces of side-wall mounted track, for example), the dimensions of the door opening, and any other factors. Record the dimensions on a freehand sketch. Plan your component dimensions; determine which parts will be inset and which will overlay others.

Backs add extra strength and rigidity. Since these components are not viewed from the side, the back can overlay the sides, bottom, and top, flush with the outer edges.

The same construction process applies to either a horizontal or a vertical module. Cut the pieces to size and sand surfaces that will remain exposed. Apply veneer tape to plywood edges where they will be visible unless you plan to paint the component. Predrill and screw, or glue and nail, the parts together. Countersink and plug the screw-holes, or set the nails and fill the holes with putty. Let the component dry, then finish as you desire.

Apply side tracks to a vertical module as described in the six-track system, so that the tracks coordinate with those mounted on the side walls. Hang the rods and shelves where you want them, and the closet is ready to use.

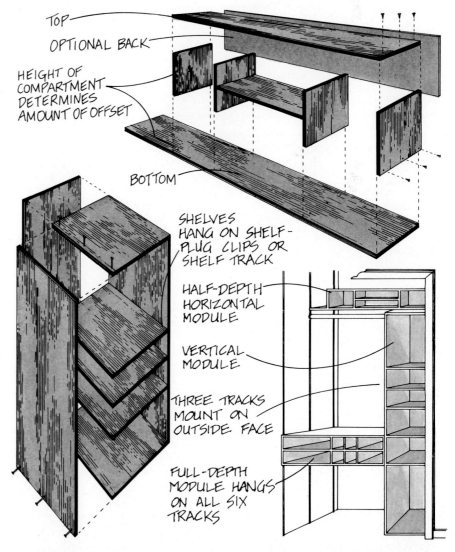

TOP

OPTIONAL BACK

HEIGHT OF COMPARTMENT DETERMINES AMOUNT OF OFFSET

BOTTOM

SHELVES HANG ON SHELF-PLUG CLIPS OR SHELF TRACK

HALF-DEPTH HORIZONTAL MODULE

VERTICAL MODULE

THREE TRACKS MOUNT ON OUTSIDE FACE

FULL-DEPTH MODULE HANGS ON ALL SIX TRACKS

Rollouts

Rollouts do what shelves do—only better. A cabinet encloses a certain amount of space. You can hang any number of shelves in it. The problem: the more shelves you hang, the less space you have between them, which means less visual and physical access to the things on them.

The rollout—essentially a platform on slides—strikes the perfect balance between capacity and accessibility. Anywhere you have or can create two parallel stationary mounting surfaces, you can build a rollout.

Form a Storage Plan. What do you want to put on the rollout? What sizes and shapes are the things you want to store there, and how heavy or light are they?

Size Up Your Space Resources. Is your space wide, or is it tall? Will you use a horizontal rollout or a vertical one?

Define the Look You Want. What do you want the visual effect to be? Do you want the rollout concealed behind existing doors, or should its finished face be exposed? Do you want to match existing cabinetry details?

Choose the Way You Want the Rollout to Work. Do you want full-extension slides, or will partial-extension slides be sufficient? Do you want a single-shelf rollout, or do you want a whole unit of shelves to slide out at once? Would you like to be able to reach things from both sides?

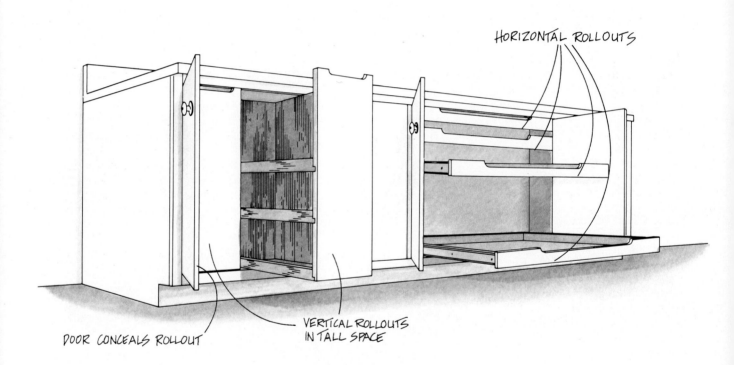

HORIZONTAL ROLLOUTS

DOOR CONCEALS ROLLOUT

VERTICAL ROLLOUTS IN TALL SPACE

Selecting Slide Hardware

Choosing slides for your rollout is the first step toward your finished product. Slides come in standard lengths from 12 inches to 36 inches. There are two basic types: partial and full extension.

Partial-extension slides consist of rollers and runner channels that work together to glide all but the last 4 inches of the roller unit beyond its enclosing space. They are relatively inexpensive, easy to install, and they support light and average loads well. Light loads (to 25 pounds) would consist of such items as small cooking utensils, spices and cereals, paper products, folded clothing and linens. Average loads (to 50 pounds) might consist of small hand-held equipment or appliances, food staples and condiments, pots, pans, and cleaning supplies.

Full-extension slides can do more for you than partial-extension slides, because their roller-runner mechanisms interlock and telescope out in sections. That means they can glide the rollout forward those extra 4 inches, giving you total access to what's on the rollout. Full-extension slides can support heavy loads (to 100 pounds—such things as counter appliances, cans, filed papers, and stereo components) and even extra-heavy loads (to 150 pounds—a microwave oven or a television, for example) extremely well. Hence their extra cost and the extra-careful preparation necessary for their installation.

Slide Mountings

Slides can be mounted in lots of
different configurations, as long as
they are fastened to stable, parallel
surfaces. The mounting surfaces
need not be existing ones; you can
create sturdy slide-mounting
surfaces where you need them
simply by adding cleats. Keep your
own storage plan and space
resources in mind as you look over
some of the options illustrated in the
schematic diagrams at right.

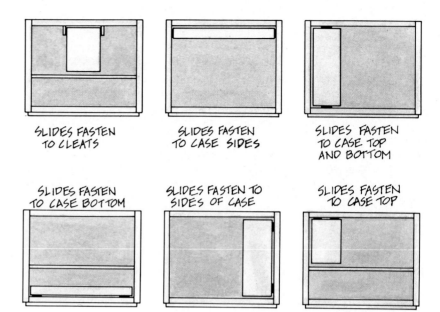

SLIDES FASTEN
TO CLEATS

SLIDES FASTEN
TO CASE SIDES

SLIDES FASTEN
TO CASE TOP
AND BOTTOM

SLIDES FASTEN
TO CASE BOTTOM

SLIDES FASTEN TO
SIDES OF CASE

SLIDES FASTEN
TO CASE TOP

Platform Designs

Your design should grow out of your
storage plan. Start the design
process by deciding what you want
to store in your space and how you
want to reach these things—from

above the platform? From both sides
of a vertical unit or from only one
side? Think about the sizes and
shapes of the items and about how
you will organize them for the most
convenient access and use.

The sketches on this page show
some basic platform shapes and
suggest some possible applications.
Let them spark your imagination to
design just the right rollouts for you.

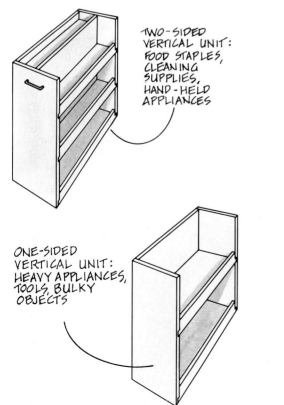

TWO-SIDED
VERTICAL UNIT:
FOOD STAPLES,
CLEANING
SUPPLIES,
HAND-HELD
APPLIANCES

DOWEL-BAR
HANGER UNIT:
LINENS, FABRICS

ONE-SIDED
VERTICAL UNIT:
HEAVY APPLIANCES,
TOOLS, BULKY
OBJECTS

FLUSH-SURFACE PLATFORM:
STEREO/TV, BUTCHER BLOCK,
MARBLE SLAB

LIP-EDGED PLATFORM:
EASY-ACCESS SHELF SURFACES,
EXTRA DRAWER SPACE

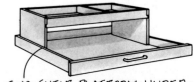

TWO-SHELF PLATFORM: UNDER-
SINK STORAGE, INSIDE BASE
CABINETRY OR CLOSETS

Rollouts

Construction Pointers

Keep the following things in mind. They can help you plan, assemble, and install successful rollouts.

Buy your slides first; different makes require different clearances and installation processes. Purchase a slide length that is less than, or exactly equal to, your cabinet's interior depth.

If there will be no door in front of the rollout, shim out your slide-mounting surface so that it is flush with the enclosure's opening.

If you're concealing rollouts behind doors, shim out the cabinet interior so that each slide-mounting surface extends a full 1/2 inch into the enclosure's opening. This allows the rollout to clear the open door.

Rollouts operate smoothly and freely only when the slide-mounting surfaces are parallel to each other. If necessary, make them parallel by inserting sandpaper or thin scrap behind the shims as you install them. Similarly, the slide-fastening surfaces on the rollout itself must also be level with each other. Be sure you position them carefully.

To plan your rollout's outside dimensions:

■ the width of a side-mounted rollout is equal to the distance between the slide-mounting surfaces less the manufacturer's required slide clearance.
■ the height of a top-and-bottom-mounted rollout is equal to the distance between the top and bottom mounting surfaces, less the manufacturer's slide clearance.
■ the body of any rollout should fit entirely within the interior depth of the cabinet.

Horizontal Rollout

Construction. Buy 3/4-inch softwood lumber of stock width for the rollout's perimeter—the front, the sides, and the back. The perimeter can be as shallow or as deep as you like. The bottom will be 1/4-inch plywood or hardboard for average loads, and up to 3/4-inch plywood for heavier loads.

Cut the front, sides, and back to length: the sides should be the same length as your slide. The front is rabbeted to 3/4 inch by 3/8 inch to accept the sides; the back butts between them. Dado the front and sides to house the bottom. To give the rollout rigidity, make the bottom overlap the back; rip it to a width equal to that of the sides above their grooves. Now sand all surfaces smooth.

Using glue and finishing nails, join the sides to the front, making sure the grooves line up. Then glue and nail the back between the sides, taking care to make their top edges flush with each other.

Now that you've assembled the perimeter, accurately measure for the bottom and cut it to size. Slip it into its grooves; make sure it seats fully in the front one.

With the rollout upside down, check it to be sure it is square. If it isn't square, push on the corners of the longer diagonal until it is. Then nail the bottom securely to the back with 1-inch box nails. Finish the rollout as desired. Mount and adjust the slides according to the manufacturer's instructions, and you're ready to install the rollout.

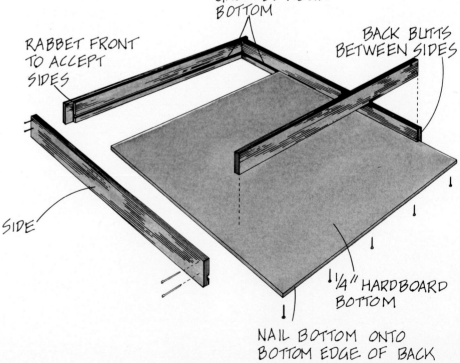

GROOVES HOUSE BOTTOM

RABBET FRONT TO ACCEPT SIDES

BACK BUTTS BETWEEN SIDES

SIDE

1/4" HARDBOARD BOTTOM

NAIL BOTTOM ONTO BOTTOM EDGE OF BACK

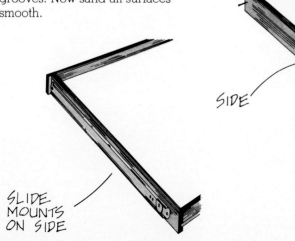

SLIDE MOUNTS ON SIDE

Vertical Rollout

Construction. Buy your materials. The front, top, bottom, back, and shelves are all made of 3/4-inch plywood; the edge lips are 1 by 3 softwood lumber. Before cutting the materials, check the clearance requirements on the slide package. Then cut the parts to size. The front and back are the same. The top is the same width as the front and back; the shelves and bottom will be 1-1/2 inches narrower than the top to account for the thickness of two edge lips per shelf surface.

Because you'll rabbet the top and bottom and dado the shelves into both the front and back to a depth of 3/8 inch, all these cross pieces are cut to the same length. Setting these pieces in grooves in the uprights will give your rollout the rigidity it needs.

With their long edges together and their inside faces up, lay the front and back on a flat work surface. Measure and mark the placement of top, shelves, and bottom; cut all rabbet and dado grooves 3/4 inch by 3/8 inch. Sand all surfaces of the rollout smooth.

To assemble, put glue in the shelf grooves; seat each shelf centered in its groove so that 3/4 inch is left at each edge for the lip. Clamp the assembly with bar clamps, or secure the unit with finishing nails through the front and back into the ends of each shelf. Glue and nail the top and bottom into place.

Cut the lumber lips to length and notch the ends so that they butt snugly between the front and back. Glue and nail the lips to the exposed edges of the shelves; then nail through the front and back faces to fasten the ends of the lips. Set the nails and putty the holes, and allow the assembly to dry. Sand, and finish as you desire. Mount the slides according to the manufacturer's instructions. The unit is ready to roll.

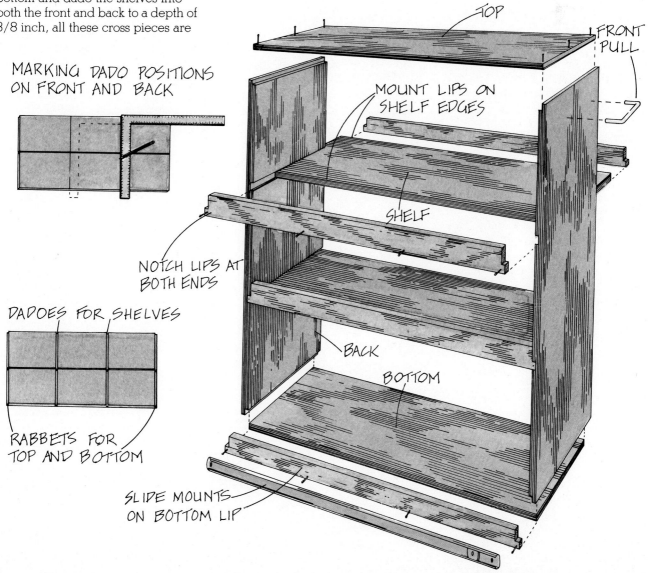

MARKING DADO POSITIONS ON FRONT AND BACK

DADOES FOR SHELVES

RABBETS FOR TOP AND BOTTOM

NOTCH LIPS AT BOTH ENDS

SLIDE MOUNTS ON BOTTOM LIP

TOP

FRONT PULL

MOUNT LIPS ON SHELF EDGES

SHELF

BACK

BOTTOM

Cases and Chests

Cases and chests, siblings in a sense, are components that do double duty. They give you new storage capacity and function as furniture at the same time. Designing your component to serve you equally well in both ways is challenging and fun. Take a moment to discover some of the options on these four pages.

Both cases and chests can be built easily and attractively out of softwood lumber or plywood, with or without face frames and backs, with or without doors, counter surfaces, and pedestals, and painted or sealed with a natural wood finish. That gives you plenty of opportunity to mix and match the elements according to your own scheme.

Design Guidelines

Where do you start? Begin in the area where you plan to place the component. Measure existing factors: wall and floor space available for use; electrical switches or outlets that may have to remain accessible; trim and furniture height-lines nearby. Record the dimensions on a freehand sketch.

Now consider these ideas: as furniture, your project should enhance the space you put it in. Plan it to be compatible with the other elements in the room in style, finish, and proportion. For instance, the height of door or window trim might suggest a pleasing height for a wall case; baseboard or toe-space

heights might guide you in determining a pedestal height for a chest-seat. You may want to add a face frame; if so, see page 90. As a storage unit, your component should be shaped by the things you plan to store there. Make a sketch, establish dimensions, purchase the materials, and you're ready to build.

Basic Lumber Case

Construction. Cut your materials to size. On the uprights, mark off placements for shelf-support holes at 1-inch or 2-inch intervals; position them in a line 3/4 inch in from the long edges of each of the uprights. These holes are for plug-type shelf clips. Drill the holes 3/8 inch deep, using a 1/4-inch drill bit; be sure to keep it perpendicular to the board's face. To mark the bit's penetration, wrap its shank at 3/8 inch with masking tape. Sand the shelves and the inside faces of the case parts, first with 80-, then with 120-grit sandpaper.

To assemble the case, set one side in position against the case top and predrill, countersink, and screw the parts together from the outside face of the upright. Repeat this process for the top and other side, and then the bottom piece, taking care to make the case square. Plug the countersunk screw-holes by putting a few drops of glue into them, inserting plugs, hammering the plugs home, and letting them dry. Then chisel the plugs not quite flush with the case sides to avoid the risk of gouging; they're easy to sand off with 80- or 120-grit paper. Finish sanding the case, the shelves, and the exposed face of the inset toe-board with 180-grit paper followed by 220-grit paper.

To mount the toe-board at the foot, screw or nail on cleating 1 inch from the face of the sides and bottom shelf as shown. Nail the board to the cleats, set the nails, and putty the

nail holes. Finish your case and shelves as desired: oil and wax make an attractive finish that is easy to apply and can be renewed as needed.

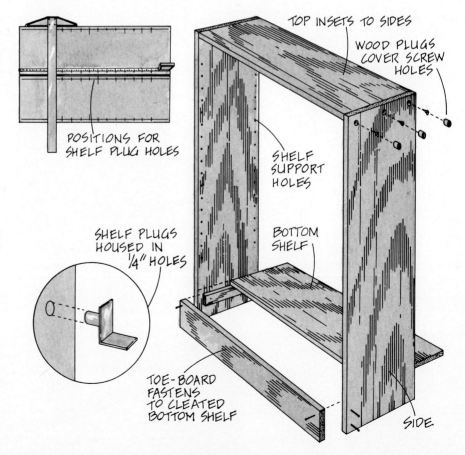

POSITIONS FOR SHELF PLUG HOLES

SHELF PLUGS HOUSED IN 1/4" HOLES

TOE-BOARD FASTENS TO CLEATED BOTTOM SHELF

TOP INSETS TO SIDES

WOOD PLUGS COVER SCREW HOLES

SHELF SUPPORT HOLES

BOTTOM SHELF

SIDE

Basic Plywood Case

Plywood gives you design options that lumber doesn't offer. Plywood is relatively inexpensive; easy to cut and fasten; resistant to warping, twisting, and cupping; and commonly available in a wide variety of surface veneers and standardized thicknesses, and in wide pieces.

On the other hand, plywood has less rigidity than lumber. It also requires more cutting. And, although plywood is a fine building material, it won't look it unless you cover its exposed edges.

These problems are easily solved, however. Adding a 1/4-inch back will give a plywood case extra strength and rigidity. Veneer tape, which you can purchase, or lumber edging, which you mill, are easy to apply to exposed edges. When you build with plywood, how your project functions and looks are very much matters of your choice.

Construction. This case uses the same basic construction process as the lumber case on the facing page with three added steps: ripping the plywood sheet to shelf widths, covering the exposed plywood edges, and mounting a 1/4-inch plywood back.

Cut your materials to size, the top and bottom pieces the same width as the uprights. At the back, inside edge of each of these parts, mill a 3/8-inch by 3/8-inch rabbet to house the back. Cut the adjustable shelves 1/2 inch narrower than the uprights. If you plan to use lumber strips for edging, rather than veneer tape, cut sufficient 1/4-inch by 3/4-inch lumber strips (or decora-tive molding) to cover the uprights' front and top edges and each of the cross-members' front edges. Apply lumber strips with glue and brads, veneer tape with contact cement; let dry. Mark and drill the shelf support holes. Sand all surfaces in the direction of the grain. For plywood, you can begin directly with 120-grit paper; be careful not sand through to the veneers below.

Assemble the case, cleat-mount the toe-board, and nail in a 1/4-inch plywood back; take care with each step to keep the case square. Sand all exposed surfaces with 180-, then 220-grit paper. Finish the case and shelves as you choose; either apply paint to paint-grade plywood, or apply plastic oil sealer or lacquer over natural or stained wood finishes. Either of these makes an attractive, durable choice.

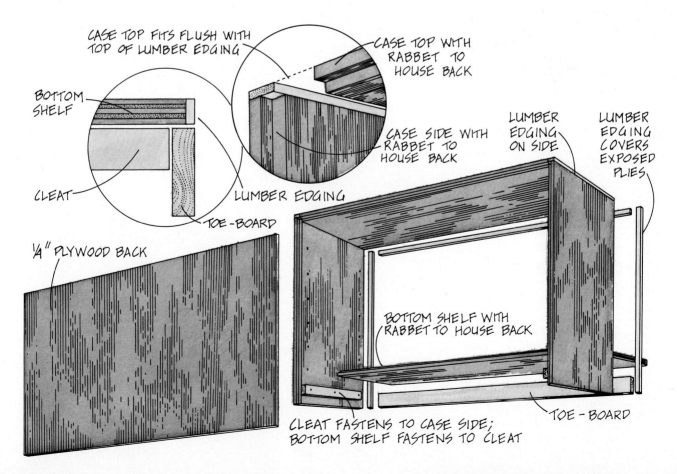

CASE TOP FITS FLUSH WITH TOP OF LUMBER EDGING

CASE TOP WITH RABBET TO HOUSE BACK

BOTTOM SHELF

CASE SIDE WITH RABBET TO HOUSE BACK

LUMBER EDGING ON SIDE

LUMBER EDGING COVERS EXPOSED PLIES

CLEAT

LUMBER EDGING

TOE-BOARD

1/4" PLYWOOD BACK

BOTTOM SHELF WITH RABBET TO HOUSE BACK

TOE-BOARD

CLEAT FASTENS TO CASE SIDE; BOTTOM SHELF FASTENS TO CLEAT

Cases and Chests

Tops, Doors, and Toes

Tops, doors, and toes make your project work and look better. How? Toes make an easy job of leveling the case when you place or install it. Doors enclose the volume, simplifying the visual effect. And tops add rigidity, cover exposed plywood edges, and create a finished counter surface all at the same time.

Still, these elements reach beyond the strictly utilitarian; each adds a special rhythm and line to your project's overall effect. The materials you select, how you join them, and how you combine the elements in your project — these are the design details that bring your craft to the sphere of art. Yet you don't need an artisan's skill or sophisticated tools to make details that delight the eye. Consider the simple options below. Use the basic construction themes and have fun concocting your own variations.

Tops

- Cut your material to size.
- Edge it using glue and nails.
- Set nail heads, putty the holes, and sand.
- Fasten the top down with counter fasteners.
- Trim out the undersurface if you choose.
- Finish the unit.

Doors

- Cut the doors to size, and make any detail cuts.
- Putty; sand all surfaces; apply any trim or moldings.
- Mount the hinges to the doors; then mount the doors in their openings.
- Apply the finish.
- Install pulls and catches.

There are three door mounting styles: overlay, lipped overlay, and flush inset. The hinge mechanisms for each type differ; choose among them according to your door mounting style first, then according to the look you want to create.

Toes

- Cut your material to size. Butt or miter lumber joints and miter or edge plywood joints.
- Cut foot details as you like.
- Assemble using glue and nails.
- Set nail heads, putty the holes, and sand.
- Finish the pedestal, then set it under your case.

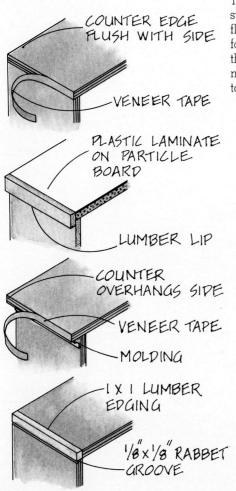

COUNTER EDGE FLUSH WITH SIDE

VENEER TAPE

PLASTIC LAMINATE ON PARTICLE BOARD

LUMBER LIP

COUNTER OVERHANGS SIDE

VENEER TAPE

MOLDING

1 X 1 LUMBER EDGING

1/8" x 1/8" RABBET GROOVE

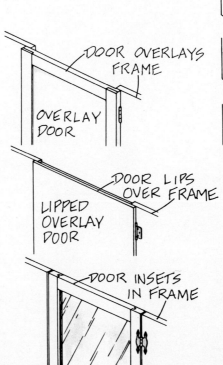

DOOR OVERLAYS FRAME

OVERLAY DOOR

DOOR LIPS OVER FRAME

LIPPED OVERLAY DOOR

DOOR INSETS IN FRAME

FLUSH INSET DOOR

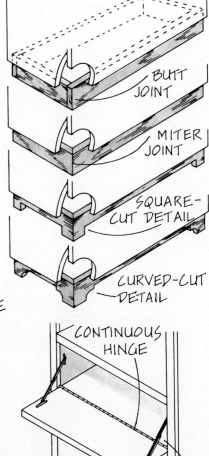

BUTT JOINT

MITER JOINT

SQUARE-CUT DETAIL

CURVED-CUT DETAIL

CONTINUOUS HINGE

FOLD-DOWN DOOR STOP

Chests

Chests are versatile, long-lived components. In fact, they're probably the oldest and most enduring storage "system."

A front-opening chest works like a low cabinet: build a face frame instead of the single plywood front in the project below, and mount doors or full-face rollouts in the opening. The key advantages to this type of chest are convenient access, since what you set on the chest-top can remain there when you get things out of it, and easy organization, since all manner of things can be stored on shelves or rollouts.

A top-opening chest, like the project shown below, functions like a big, deep, hinge-lidded box. This is the easiest type of chest to build. Design yours as a coffee table, or tailor its dimensions to a size you can sit on or nap on.

Use the interior space to store large, regularly shaped things, or items that stack easily. Bagged pet food, canning kettles and jars, backpacks, sleeping bags, and camping equipment, slide screen and projector, boxed items and seasonal decorations, blankets and pillows stow naturally in lidded chests. Installing friction-type lid supports will make your chest safer and easier to use.

Construction. Cut your materials to size. Make both sides the same, and make the back the same height as the sides. The front is 1-1/2 inches narrower than the sides and back; the bottom and lid are both 1-1/2 inches narrower than the sides. Make the bottom, back, front, and lid all equal in length to each other. Then cut two pieces of 3/4-inch cove molding, each to the length of the lid. With contact cement, apply veneer tape to the chest eges that will remain exposed—the front, lip, and back edges of both side pieces, and the top edge of the back.

Now you're ready to assemble. Predrill, countersink, and screw the back, sides, and front together, taking care to keep the butt joints square and flush. Measure and mark the placement for the chest's bottom, so that a 1/4-inch-deep recess is formed below it; this will house the pedestal, which you'll build separately. Position the bottom, predrill, and countersink. Screw the bottom to the sides, back, and front. Attach the cove molding to the front's top edge, using glue and finishing nails. Then repeat the process for the lid's front edge.

Mount a continuous hinge to the lid, then fasten it to the back.

Give the lid extra support by cleating the sides with 1 by 2 strips; screw them in 3/4 inch below the top edge. Plug all the countersunk holes; when dry, chisel and sand the plugs flush with the surface. Working in the direction of the grain, sand all surfaces; first use 120-grit, then 180-, and 220-grit sandpaper. Build the pedestal to suit (see opposite page), and finish it along with the rest. Hand-rub 400-grit wet/dry sandpaper over oil, then wax for a very glassy finish.

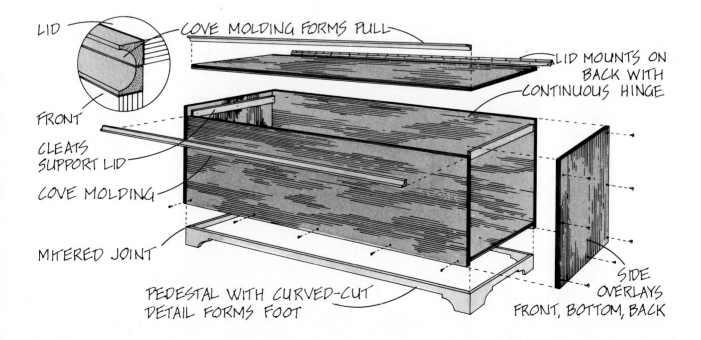

LID

COVE MOLDING FORMS PULL

LID MOUNTS ON BACK WITH CONTINUOUS HINGE

FRONT

CLEATS SUPPORT LID

COVE MOLDING

MITERED JOINT

PEDESTAL WITH CURVED-CUT DETAIL FORMS FOOT

SIDE OVERLAYS FRONT, BOTTOM, BACK

Racks

Racks are rough constructions—sturdy but not elegant. Two distinguishing traits describe their real beauty—speed of construction and durability. They differ from the other projects in this book in that they are less finished—you use inexpensive construction materials, leave plywood edges and screw-heads exposed, and need apply no finish. Build and install any of them in a day, then take advantage of their serviceable strength for years to come.

Lumber and plywood work in concert here. The concept is this: the lumber forms the skeleton, or frame, and the plywood forms the skin, or sheathing; the frames support the sheathing and the sheathing stiffens the frames. The result is a lot of sturdy storage surface using light, simple construction techniques.

If your skills are still developing, hone them on a rough construction project. Basement, attic, garage, or carport sites might welcome the improvement and you'll be ready to take on other component projects with new confidence.

Hanging Racks

Either exposed or unexposed joists and rafters make natural surfaces for mounting hanging racks. In the garage or carport, mount these racks over the hood of the car to put that space into active service. Hanging racks are also excellent components in basements where water seepage occurs; they can hang close to the floor, yet not touch it. The verticals can be as short or as long as you like. For more shelf surface on a rack, make longer verticals, add intermediate cross-members, and insert plywood shelves.

The same simple construction techniques are also used in building floor-standing shelves.

Construction. Measure the space you plan to use and record the dimensions on a freehand sketch. Note the existing structure—distance between joists or rafters, for instance. Plan to space your hangers 32 inches to 36 inches apart. In an attic space, where the roof slope will make one set of verticals shorter than the other, determine the lengths they need to be. Mounted on floor or ceiling joists, the verticals will be of equal length.

Cut 1 by 4 softwood to length, two verticals and one horizontal for each hanger. Predrill and screw or nail the cross-member to the face of the verticals, squaring each corner with a combination or framing square. Locate and mark the mounting positions on the sides of the rafters or joists, making sure that each hanging frame will be lined up with the next. With a hammer, blunt the points of the nails (so they won't split the wood), start them at the top of each vertical, and nail the frames in place.

Cut the shelving to size out of 3/4-inch plywood; the shelf surface should be as wide as the opening between verticals, less 1/8 inch for clearance, and can be cut long enough to overhang the frames by a foot at either end. Position the shelving and nail it down in one or two places along the length of each cross-member.

If the space has a finished ceiling, you can still mount hanging racks. Lag-bolt lengths of 2 by 4 to the joists or rafters and side-nail the racks to these 2 by 4 cleats.

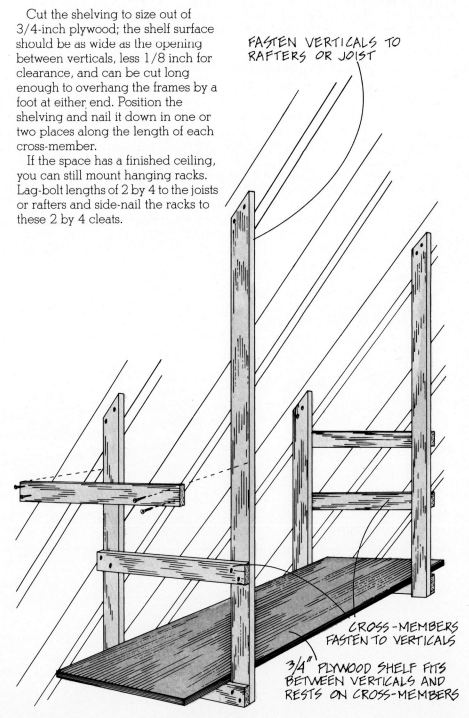

FASTEN VERTICALS TO RAFTERS OR JOIST

CROSS-MEMBERS FASTEN TO VERTICALS

3/4" PLYWOOD SHELF FITS BETWEEN VERTICALS AND RESTS ON CROSS-MEMBERS

Floor-Standing Shelves

Floor-standing shelves are a variation on hanging racks; refer to those construction steps at left. Build support frames out of 1 by 4 softwood lumber; make one for each 3 feet of shelf length you plan, not including the 1-foot overhang you can allow at each outside edge. Cut the lumber to length. Predrill and screw or nail the cross-members to the uprights, making sure the joints are square.

To assemble the unit, space the frames according to your plan and tack them together with a nailer made of a length of 1 by 4 nailed across the back at the frame's top edges. Nail another 1 by 4 twelve inches above the floor, fastening it securely to each frame's edge. Stand the assembly up in place; through the 1 by 4 nailers at the back, fasten the unit to the wall. Measure and cut your shelves to size out of 3/4-inch plywood. Position and nail them securely to the cross-members, squaring the frames to the shelves as you proceed. When you're finished, they're ready to go to work.

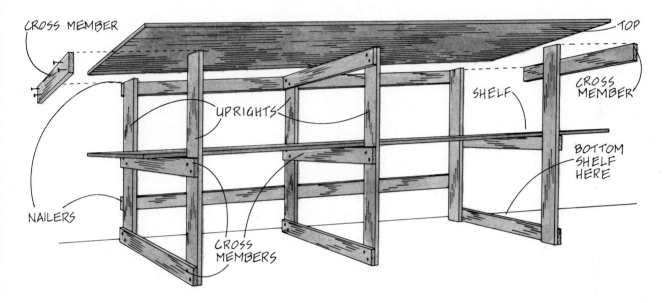

Pipe-Supported Shelves

Shelves supported by pipes are easy to build and will carry a great deal of weight. If you plan your design ahead, you can have your materials cut to size where you purchase them. Shelves of 3/4-inch plywood up to 24 inches wide will carry average loads well; for very heavy loads, make the shelves no more than 18 inches wide. You'll install one 1/2-inch pipe support in every other stud; plan to have pipe lengths cut the width of the shelf, plus 2-1/2 inches—the depth to which the pipe penetrates the stud.

Your wall's stud spacing will determine the length of shelf you can use. Where studs are located 2 feet on center, drill a hole in each stud to house a pipe support; four pipes will support an 8-foot shelf. If studs are on 16-inch centers, drill and house pipe in every other stud; three pipes will support an 8-foot shelf.

Construction. First, locate the studs and mark the ones you'll use with an "X." Measure and mark the pipe support placements on the center of each working stud; take care to make the supports of each shelf in the same level plane and level with the floor. Centered in the stud face, and square to the wall surface, drill a hole 2-1/2 inches deep for each pipe support (mark the drill bit's shank with a felt pen or piece of tape). The hole should just barely house the pipe, so that you have to lightly hammer it home. Install the pipe lengths, lay the shelving over each support, and fasten it from underneath using pipe brackets.

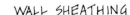
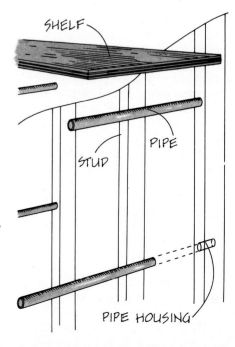

Tools, Techniques, and Tips

Materials

On the following pages are guidelines for the techniques you will need to build the projects in this book, as well as basic information on tools, materials, hardware, spans and loads, joints, and reinforcing.

A description of wood and wood products can be only an introduction to their rich variety of tone, color, working and finishing characteristics, grain patterns and variations, defects, strengths, and vulnerabilities. The best education, and the most enjoyable one, is in the lumberyard itself. There you can see your choices, select just the material you want, and learn a great deal in the process. Ask questions, explore, take stock out of the racks and examine it for defects and special beauty. The guidelines below give you a starting point—the best part of learning about wood is left for you.

Lumber	Plywood	Particle Board and Hardboard
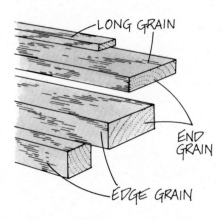		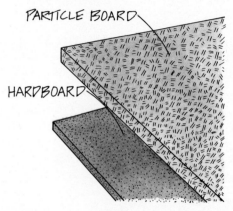

Lumber

■ Of all wood products, lumber has the greatest rigidity and strength. Hardwoods, such as birch, oak, and cherry, are stronger and more durable than softwoods—fir and pine, for example.

■ Lumber is sold in stock dimensions of thickness, width, and length, which means you can buy just the amount you need, plus a little extra for error. If you design your project using stock sizes, you can arrange it so the only milling required will be crosscutting the parts to length. At the lumberyard, you'll ask for lumber by *nominal* dimensions—1 by 4 or 2 by 2, for instance. But remember that, as sold, lumber has been surfaced to standard finish dimensions, which are smaller. In designing your project, use the *actual* sizes.

■ Softwoods in general are easy to work, and usually you need to predrill only for screws, not for nails. Hardwoods need to be predrilled for both nails and screws.

■ For gluing and fastening, face grain and edge grain afford the most strength, end grain the least.

Plywood

■ Plywood is made of layers (plies) of wood glued together with their grains running in alternating directions. Plywood faces may be made of either hardwood or softwood veneer.

■ Plywood is typically sold in 4 by 8 sheets, which gives you great range in designing the size and shape of your project. But buying in sheets means you'll have to do more cutting—both ripping and cross-cutting. Plywood ranges in thickness from 1/8 inch to 1-1/8 inches; for projects like those in this book, the most commonly used thicknesses are 1/4 inch, 1/2 inch, and 3/4 inch.

■ Most plywoods are made up with interior plies of softwood, so you don't need pilot holes for nails, but you'll need them for screws.

■ Plywood is a fine building material; but to give a plywood project its best appearance, you'll want to conceal exposed plies with edging (see page 85). Take care in sanding any plywood, so that you don't sand right through the face; hardwood surface veneers, in particular, are thin.

Particle Board and Hardboard

■ Particle board and hardboard are made of wood chips or fibers glued together in random directions and compressed.

■ These materials are less expensive than lumber and plywood. They are sold in 4 by 8 sheets. Hardboard comes in 1/8-inch and 1/4-inch thicknesses. Particle board comes in thicknesses from 1/4 inch to 3/4 inch; it is also available in a range of standard shelving widths, sometimes with a finished front edge. Particle board comes in different grades. Under-layment grade has a rough surface and gives a coarse appearance. Industrial grade, by contrast, is dense and smooth, and takes paint well; it is a better product for the projects in this book.

■ Because hardboard and particle board have no continuous grain direction, they're tricky to fasten well. The binding glues are abrasive and are apt to dull your cutting tools. You'll need to predrill particle board for screws but not for nails; you may be able to fasten hardboard without predrilling, depending on whether it's been tempered.

Spans and Loads

Shelving shouldn't sag or bend under the weight of a load. The guidelines and chart on this page will help you select the appropriate materials for your project. Note that there are a number of ways to deal with a too-heavy load: you can reinforce the shelf, change the material you construct it of, choose a thicker or wider piece of stock, or shorten the span. The general guideline is: the thinner, the narrower in width, and the longer the piece of stock, the more apt it is to bend.

Materials

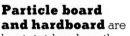

Lumber is the most rigid material and therefore least apt to bend under loads.

Plywood is less rigid than lumber and thus more apt to bend.

Particle board and hardboard are least rigid and are thus apt to bend or even break under loads.

Load Types

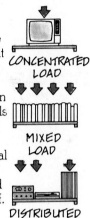

CONCENTRATED LOAD

MIXED LOAD

DISTRIBUTED LOAD

In designing a shelf, consider not only the weight but also how it will be distributed, and select a shelf design, a construction method, and materials that have sufficient rigidity to avoid sagging. The potential for sagging will vary with the way the load is placed on the shelf.

Ways to Reinforce a Sagging Shelf

Be conservative in deciding the length of shelf spans; if there is a possibility of sagging, use one of the reinforcing methods shown here.

LUMBER

MID-SPAN SUPPORT

CLEATS

Apply lumber to one or both long edges.

Add mid-span supports as needed.

Add support around shelf edges.

Load Capacities

Light load ■
10 to 15 pounds.
Example: towels.

Average load ●
15 to 25 pounds.
Example: mix of canned and boxed food staples.

Heavy load ▲
25 to 50 pounds.
Example: records.

Reinforce **R**
You'll need to reinforce a shelf of these dimensions.

Length									
1″ Lumber	**12″**	**18″**	**24″**	**30″**	**36″**	**42″**	**48″**	**54″**	**60″**
4″ Wide	▲	▲	●	●	■	■	R	R	R
6″	▲	▲	▲	●	●	■	■	R	R
8″	▲	▲	▲	▲	●	●	■	■	R
10″	▲	▲	▲	▲	▲	●	●	■	■
12″	▲	▲	▲	▲	▲	▲	●	●	■
3/4″ Plywood									
4″ Wide	▲	●	●	●	■	■	R	R	R
8″	▲	▲	▲	●	●	■	■	R	R
12″	▲	▲	▲	▲	▲	●	■	■	R
16″	▲	▲	▲	▲	▲	●	●	■	■
20″	▲	▲	▲	▲	▲	▲	●	●	■
24″	▲	▲	▲	▲	▲	▲	▲	●	●
3/4″ Particle Board									
4″ Wide	▲	●	●	■	■	R	R	R	R
8″	▲	▲	●	●	■	■	R	R	R
12″	▲	▲	▲	●	●	■	■	R	R
16″	▲	▲	▲	▲	●	●	■	■	R
20″	▲	▲	▲	▲	▲	●	●	■	■
24″	▲	▲	▲	▲	▲	▲	●	●	■

Sizing Up Your Space

Sizing up your space is the first order of business. Using graph paper to help you draw your room in proportion, sketch the major features of the area where the component will go. Measure and record the height, width, and depth of these features (walls, door and window openings) on your freehand sketch. Work your way down to the details (trim, and so forth). The more you know about the space before you lay out your project, the better. The easiest measuring tool for most places is a 3/4-inch-wide, spring-loaded, lockable steel tape 12 or 16 feet long. If you're measuring a spot where you can't read the tape, lock the tape in its extended position and then take it out to read it.

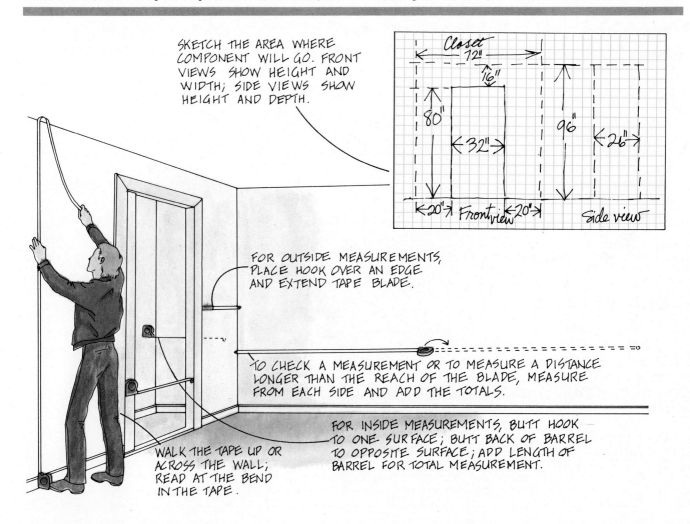

SKETCH THE AREA WHERE COMPONENT WILL GO. FRONT VIEWS SHOW HEIGHT AND WIDTH; SIDE VIEWS SHOW HEIGHT AND DEPTH.

FOR OUTSIDE MEASUREMENTS, PLACE HOOK OVER AN EDGE AND EXTEND TAPE BLADE.

TO CHECK A MEASUREMENT OR TO MEASURE A DISTANCE LONGER THAN THE REACH OF THE BLADE, MEASURE FROM EACH SIDE AND ADD THE TOTALS.

FOR INSIDE MEASUREMENTS, BUTT HOOK TO ONE SURFACE; BUTT BACK OF BARREL TO OPPOSITE SURFACE; ADD LENGTH OF BARREL FOR TOTAL MEASUREMENT.

WALK THE TAPE UP OR ACROSS THE WALL; READ AT THE BEND IN THE TAPE.

Plumb, Flat, and Parallel

Although they may look perfectly all right to your eye, walls aren't necessarily plumb (truly vertical), flat, or parallel to one another. Before you cut the pieces of your project, check the walls. If you need to make a correction, either shim out the wall surfaces so they're even, or add or subtract shelf length to solve the problem.

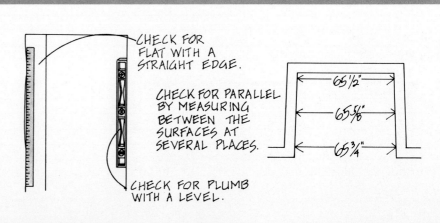

CHECK FOR FLAT WITH A STRAIGHT EDGE.

CHECK FOR PARALLEL BY MEASURING BETWEEN THE SURFACES AT SEVERAL PLACES.

CHECK FOR PLUMB WITH A LEVEL.

Layout and Cutting List

Layout

Lay out your project on a fresh piece of graph or tracing paper. Draw as many views as you need to visualize the size of each part and its relationship to the whole component. Make your sketches large, simple, and clear. Take the time to erase and resketch—correcting a mistake on a sketch is easy, inexpensive, and painless; correcting a mistake on your component is not. Your layout is complete when you've determined and recorded on it:

the type of material you'll use for each part: lumber, plywood, particle board or hardboard, and its stock thickness.

the size of each part: its width and length.

how it connects to other parts: will it butt, or rabbet, or dado into them, for example?

how all the parts work together to form the whole: which parts overlap others, and which parts fit between others.

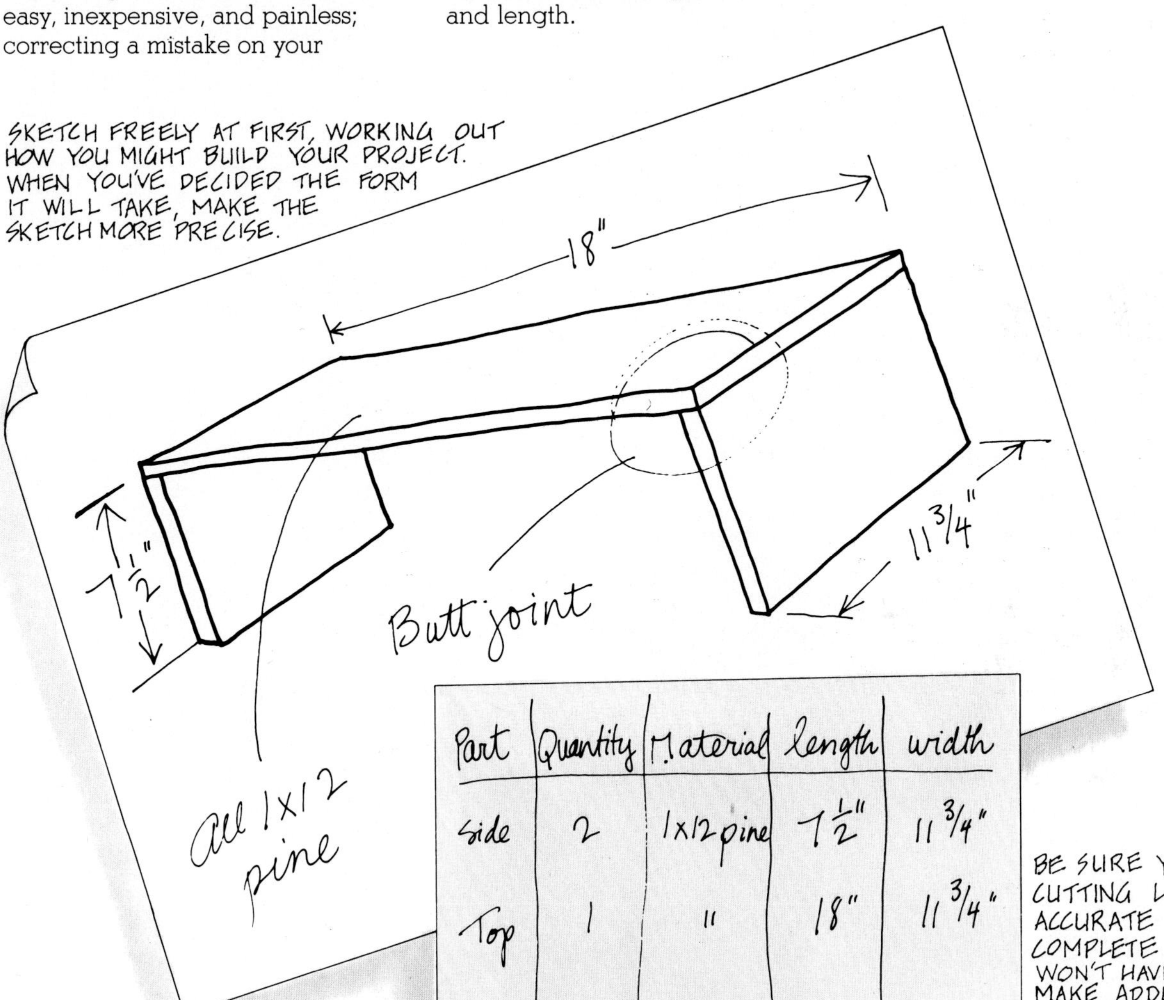

SKETCH FREELY AT FIRST, WORKING OUT HOW YOU MIGHT BUILD YOUR PROJECT. WHEN YOU'VE DECIDED THE FORM IT WILL TAKE, MAKE THE SKETCH MORE PRECISE.

18"

11 3/4"

7 1/2"

Butt joint

All 1x12 pine

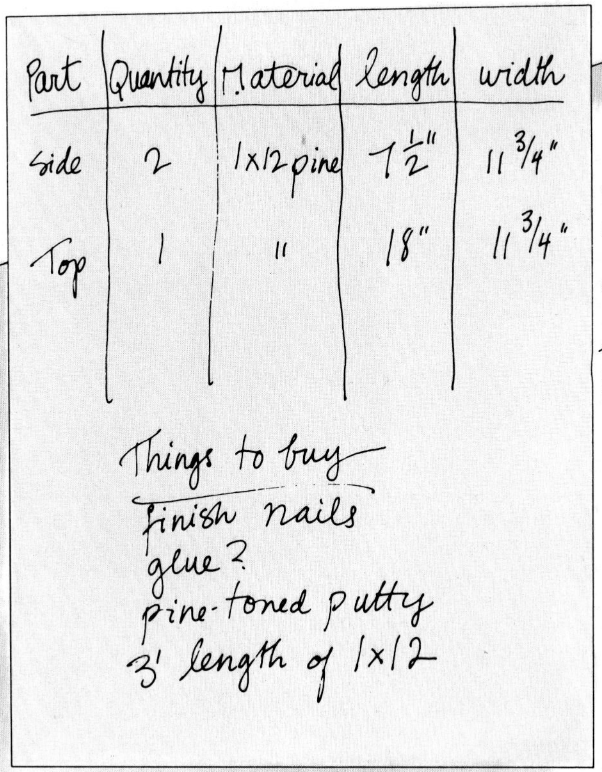

Part	Quantity	Material	length	width
Side	2	1x12 pine	7 1/2"	11 3/4"
Top	1	"	18"	11 3/4"

BE SURE YOUR CUTTING LIST IS ACCURATE AND COMPLETE. YOU WON'T HAVE TO MAKE ADDITIONAL TRIPS TO HARDWARE STORE AND LUMBER-YARD, AND PURCHAS-ING AND MILLING WILL BE EASY.

Things to buy
finish nails
glue?
pine-toned putty
3' length of 1x12

Cutting List

Use your layout sketch to make up a cutting list. From that list figure the amount of material you need to purchase. Mistakes do happen, so purchase a little more of each type than you think you'll need. Add to your shopping list hardware and any other supplies (such as putty, dowels, and sandpaper) that you may need for your project. If you'll need any new tools, jot them down, too.

Cuts and Joints

Cutting the material to size is a two-step process. The general rule of thumb is this: first, rip the materials to width, then cross-cut the pieces to length. To get the most out of the material, rip the widest pieces first; then rip the narrower pieces out of the remainder. Follow the same order for crosscutting, starting with the longest pieces.

Saw Blades

Saw blades are specially designed to make specific types of cuts in different types of materials. Since using unsuitable blades can waste materials and put stress on your tools, you'll want to choose the right blade for the job. Keep blades sharp: it's a safer practice; and sharp blades are more likely to produce the clean cuts and good joints you want. And remember, whenever you change a blade, unplug the tool first.

Saws

Accurate cuts produce tight, attractive joints. Stationary power tools like the radial arm saw and the table saw are highly prized shop tools because they yield the most precise cuts. But a portable circular saw, when you use it well, is also an accurate milling tool. It will make the most precise cuts when you suit the blade to the material, support the material on a cutting table or a portable work bench, and use rip and crosscut guides to cut your material to size. The illustrations below show how to make both of the cutting guides.

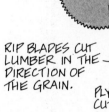

CROSSCUT BLADES CUT LUMBER ACROSS THE DIRECTION OF THE GRAIN.

RIP BLADES CUT LUMBER IN THE DIRECTION OF THE GRAIN.

PLYWOOD BLADES CUT PLYWOOD IN ANY DIRECTION.

PLANER BLADES CUT VERY SMOOTHLY IN ALL WOOD MATERIALS IN ANY DIRECTION.

COMBINATION BLADES CUT LUMBER AND PLYWOOD OR OTHER WOOD SHEET MATERIALS IN ANY DIRECTION.

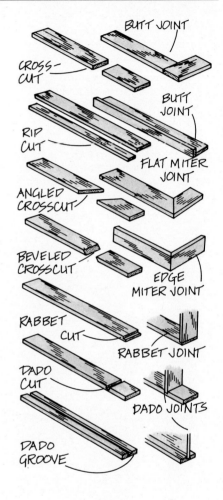

BUTT JOINT

CROSS-CUT

BUTT JOINT

RIP CUT

FLAT MITER JOINT

ANGLED CROSSCUT

BEVELED CROSSCUT

EDGE MITER JOINT

RABBET CUT

RABBET JOINT

DADO CUT

DADO JOINTS

DADO GROOVE

RIP GUIDE

¼" PLYWOOD (AT LEAST AS WIDE AS SOLE OF SAW)

7 SCREWS 15" APART. (OUTSIDE SCREWS 1" FROM EACH END.)

8' LONG 1 X 2

CROSSCUT GUIDE

LONG LEG

SHORT LEG

GLUE AND SCREW TWO PIECES OF 1 X 4 SO THAT THEY FORM AN ACCURATE (90°) ANGLE.

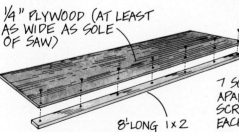

TO TRIM GUIDE, CLAMP AT BOTH ENDS. WITH SOLE OF SAW TIGHT AGAINST 1 X 2, RIP PLYWOOD TO WIDTH.

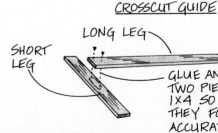

CLAMP T-SQUARE TO THE WORK. KEEPING THE SOLE OF THE SAW SNUG TO THE LONG LEG, CROSS-CUT THROUGH THE WORK AND THE SHORT LEG IN ONE PASS.

TO USE GUIDE, LINE UP SHORT LEG WITH CUTTING MARK; CLAMP AND CUT.

Detail Milling and Edging

Routing

Routers do detail milling: rabbets, dadoes, grooves, flush-trimming, and shaping straight or curved edges. You can mount your router under a bench-top table as a stationary shaper, and unmount it to use as a portable detail milling tool as well. In either case, these guidelines apply:

■ Unplug the tool before changing cutter bits.
■ Tighten bits thoroughly to prevent their wandering during the cut.
■ Turn the router on *before* starting the cutter into the work.
■ Double-check the cutter depth setting by running a test cut on a piece of scrap.

Router bits. Many bits have both roller bearings and carbide cutting edges; these bits give you the best cuts for the longest time. All cutters are designed to make a crisp, finished edge that needs no sanding.

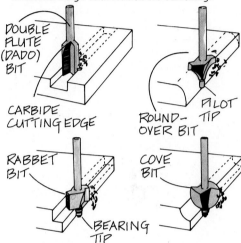

DOUBLE FLUTE (DADO) BIT

CARBIDE CUTTING EDGE

ROUND-OVER BIT

PILOT TIP

RABBET BIT

COVE BIT

BEARING TIP

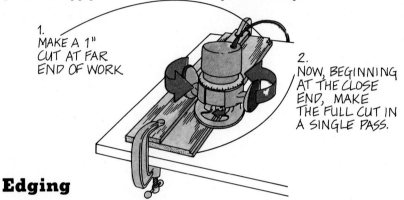

1. MAKE A 1" CUT AT FAR END OF WORK

2. NOW, BEGINNING AT THE CLOSE END, MAKE THE FULL CUT IN A SINGLE PASS.

Edging

EDGING WITH NARROW LUMBER STRIPS

1. RIP LUMBER TO 1/4" BY 3/4" STRIPS; CUT TO LENGTH. PREDRILL IF NECESSARY.

2. APPLY GLUE TO EDGE OF PART.

3. NAIL STRIP TO EDGE OF PART. THEN SET HEADS, PUTTY, AND SAND WHEN DRY.

EDGING WITH STOCK LUMBER

1. FOR HARDWOOD LUMBER, DRILL PILOT HOLES FOR NAILS; FOR SOFTWOOD, LIGHTLY TAP IN NAILS TO START THEM. APPLY GLUE, POSITION EDGING, AND DRIVE NAILS HOME.

2. SET NAIL HEADS.

3. PUTTY NAIL HOLES AND SAND WHEN DRY.

EDGING WITH VENEER TAPE

1. APPLY A COAT OF CONTACT CEMENT TO TAPE, AND TWO COATS TO PART'S EDGE.

PUSH PINS HOLD TAPE DOWN FOR GLUING

2. WHEN CEMENT IS TACKY, APPLY TAPE TO PART SO THAT IT OVERHANGS ALL EDGES.

3. TO TRIM OVER-HANG, MAKE A FEW PASSES ALONG BOTH EDGES AT A 45° ANGLE.

4. USE A RAZOR KNIFE TO CUT OFF ENDS OF TAPE FLUSH.

5. PEEL AWAY OVERHANG.

Drilling and Fastening

Drilling

Electric drills in general, and variable-speed types in particular, are versatile shop tools. They bore holes, predrill pilot holes, countersink screw-heads, cut plugs, and even drive screws. With the help of accessories, they'll do other jobs too.

HOLD DRILL BIT TO YOUR NAIL UNTIL YOU FIND ONE JUST SMALLER THAN THE NAIL'S SHANK.

NAIL   DRILL BIT

DRILL BIT   SCREW

TO SIZE THE BIT, HOLD THE SCREW BEHIND ONE OR MORE BITS UNTIL YOU CAN SEE ONLY THE THREADS, NOT THE SHANK. THAT'S THE BIT TO USE.

Predrilling. To avoid splitting the wood, you should predrill pilot holes for screws and sometimes nails (see page 80). First select the screw or nail appropriate to your project, then choose the bit to match. For nails, drill the holes in the outside piece and start the nails by lightly tapping them into the holes. Apply glue, position the boards so they are flush and tight, and hammer in the nails. Set the heads and putty the holes. For screws, if you plan to cover the screw heads, countersink and pilot-drill in one step.

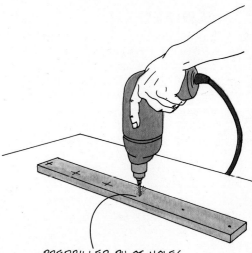

PREDRILLED PILOT HOLES EASE THE NAIL'S ENTRY SO THAT YOU DON'T RISK SPLITTING THE WOOD.

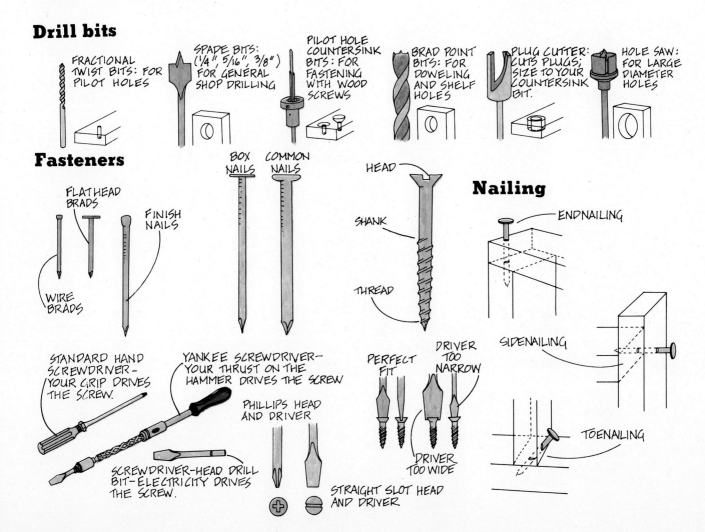

Drill bits

FRACTIONAL TWIST BITS: FOR PILOT HOLES

SPADE BITS: (1/4", 5/16", 3/8") FOR GENERAL SHOP DRILLING

PILOT HOLE COUNTERSINK BITS: FOR FASTENING WITH WOOD SCREWS

BRAD POINT BITS: FOR DOWELING AND SHELF HOLES

PLUG CUTTER: CUTS PLUGS; SIZE TO YOUR COUNTERSINK BIT.

HOLE SAW: FOR LARGE DIAMETER HOLES

Fasteners

FLAT HEAD BRADS

FINISH NAILS

WIRE BRADS

BOX NAILS

COMMON NAILS

HEAD

SHANK

THREAD

STANDARD HAND SCREWDRIVER - YOUR GRIP DRIVES THE SCREW.

YANKEE SCREWDRIVER - YOUR THRUST ON THE HAMMER DRIVES THE SCREW

SCREWDRIVER-HEAD DRILL BIT - ELECTRICITY DRIVES THE SCREW.

PHILLIPS HEAD AND DRIVER

STRAIGHT SLOT HEAD AND DRIVER

PERFECT FIT

DRIVER TOO NARROW

DRIVER TOO WIDE

Nailing

ENDNAILING

SIDENAILING

TOENAILING

Gluing, Clamping, and Assembly

Gluing

Use household white glue or an aliphatic resin glue. Both plywood edges and the end grain of lumber drink it. Quench the thirst by putting on a precoat of glue a few minutes before spreading an even layer of glue on each part where surfaces will join. A little glue should squeeze out of the joint as it seats; experience will quickly teach you how much to use. Overgluing the joint doesn't make it stronger—it just makes cleaning up harder. Let all excess glue dry, then remove it carefully with a scraper.

Clamping

Clamps are essential. At nearly every stage of your project's construction, you'll want to put a clamp to work.

SPREAD AN EVEN LAYER OF GLUE ON EACH PART WHERE SURFACES WILL JOIN.

QUARTER-ROUND

SCRAPE EXCESS GLUE AT JOINT WHEN THOROUGHLY DRY.

FACE-FRAME CLAMP

SPRING CLAMP

C-CLAMP

HAND-SCREW CLAMP

PIPE CLAMP

Assembly

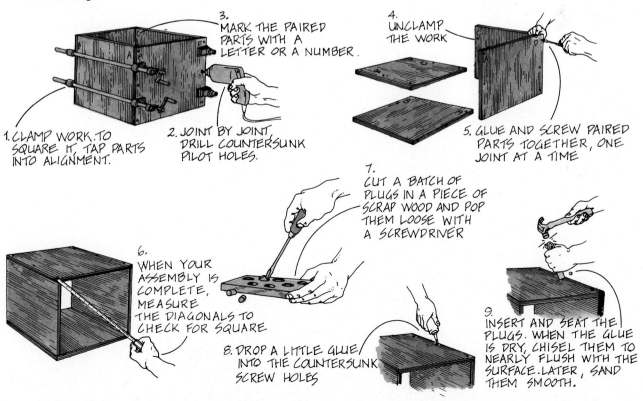

3. MARK THE PAIRED PARTS WITH A LETTER OR A NUMBER.

4. UNCLAMP THE WORK

1. CLAMP WORK TO SQUARE IT, TAP PARTS INTO ALIGNMENT.

2. JOINT BY JOINT, DRILL COUNTERSUNK PILOT HOLES.

5. GLUE AND SCREW PAIRED PARTS TOGETHER, ONE JOINT AT A TIME

7. CUT A BATCH OF PLUGS IN A PIECE OF SCRAP WOOD AND POP THEM LOOSE WITH A SCREWDRIVER

6. WHEN YOUR ASSEMBLY IS COMPLETE, MEASURE THE DIAGONALS TO CHECK FOR SQUARE

8. DROP A LITTLE GLUE INTO THE COUNTERSUNK SCREW HOLES

9. INSERT AND SEAT THE PLUGS. WHEN THE GLUE IS DRY, CHISEL THEM TO NEARLY FLUSH WITH THE SURFACE. LATER, SAND THEM SMOOTH.

Doors and Drawers

There are three ways to mount door and drawer faces: overlaid, lipped, and flush. Which one you choose will determine the type of hardware you use to mount them, the size you cut them, and the particular detail milling you do. So decide on the mounting style first, purchase the hardware, plan your cutting list, and then mill the parts.

Doors

To make any pair of doors, measure the width and height of the opening. Cut and fit as one piece, then rip it in half to get a matched pair of doors with just the right amount of clearance. Putty the edges as needed, and finish-sand. Mount a pair of hinges on each door, position the doors over the opening, and screw the hinges to the frames. Mount pulls and, unless you used self-closing hinges, catches.

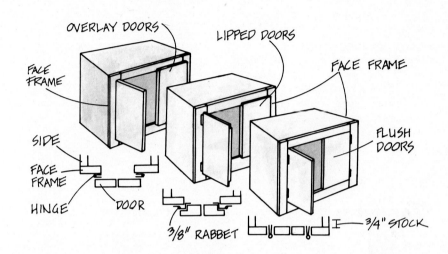

OVERLAY DOORS

LIPPED DOORS

FACE FRAME

FACE FRAME

SIDE

FLUSH DOORS

FACE FRAME

HINGE

DOOR

3/8" RABBET

3/4" STOCK

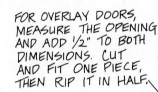

FOR OVERLAY DOORS, MEASURE THE OPENING AND ADD 1/2" TO BOTH DIMENSIONS. CUT AND FIT ONE PIECE, THEN RIP IT IN HALF.

y $y+\frac{1}{2}$ X $X+\frac{1}{2}$

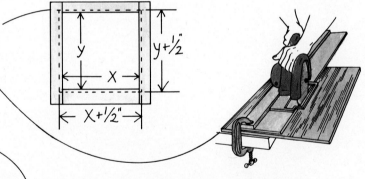

FOR LIPPED DOORS, MEASURE AS FOR OVERLAY DOORS. THEN RABBET THE OUTSIDE EDGES 3/8" × 3/8" SO THAT THE ROUTER DOESN'T SPLINTER OUT THE CORNERS, MAKE THE SHORT CUT AT THE FAR END FIRST, THEN MAKE A FULL PASS, BEGINNING AT THE OTHER END. RIP IN HALF TO FORM THE PAIR.

FOR FLUSH DOORS, MEASURE OPENING AND SUBTRACT 1/16" FROM BOTH DIMENSIONS. CUT ONE PIECE TO THAT SIZE. FIT THE DOOR, USING A BLOCK PLANE. YOU'LL PROBABLY TAKE OFF ANOTHER 1/16" FROM BOTH DIMENSIONS FOR A GOOD FIT. HOLD BLOCK PLANE DIAGONALLY TO THE WORK, NOT HEAD-ON TO IT. THEN RIP THE PIECE IN HALF.

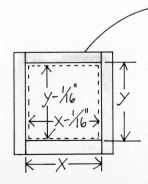

$Y-\frac{1}{16}$ $X-\frac{1}{16}$ Y X

Drawers

To make a drawer, use the construction steps for rollouts, pages 70–72. Purchase the slides first, then plan the unit's dimensions according to slide clearance allowances and the milling considerations detailed here.

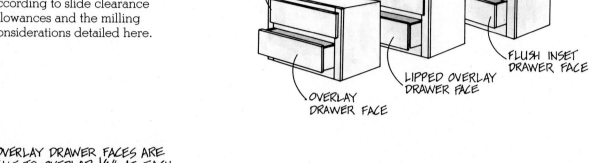

FACE FRAME

OVERLAY DRAWER FACE

LIPPED OVERLAY DRAWER FACE

FLUSH INSET DRAWER FACE

OVERLAY DRAWER FACES ARE CUT TO OVERLAP 1/4" AT EACH EDGE THAT TOUCHES THE FRAME. BUILD THE DRAWER (OR ROLLOUT PLATFORM) SO THAT THE FRONT BUTTS BE-TWEEN THE SIDES. THEN FROM THE INSIDE OF THE DRAWER BODY, SCREW THE FINISHED FACE TO THE FALSE FRONT.

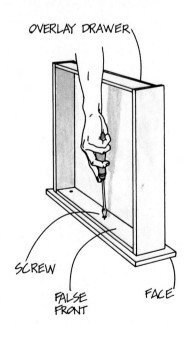

OVERLAY DRAWER

SCREW

FALSE FRONT

FACE

FLUSH INSET DRAWER FACES ARE CUT TO SIZE SO THAT THEY WILL FIT BETWEEN THE FRAME PIECES WITH 1/16" CLEARANCE. MAKE THE RABBETS WIDE ENOUGH TO HOUSE THE SIDES AND COVER THE SLIDES.

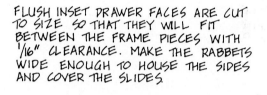
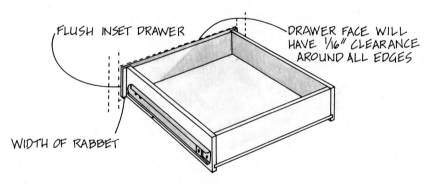

FLUSH INSET DRAWER

DRAWER FACE WILL HAVE 1/16" CLEARANCE AROUND ALL EDGES

WIDTH OF RABBET

LIPPED OVERLAY DRAWER FACES ARE CUT TO SIZE JUST AS OVERLAY FACES ARE, BUT THEY ARE FASTENED DIRECTLY TO THE DRAWER OR PLATFORM SIDES. MAKE EACH RABBET WIDE ENOUGH TO ACCOUNT FOR THE SIDE'S THICKNESS, THE REQUIRED SLIDE CLEARANCE, AND THE 1/4" LIP THAT OVER-LAPS THE FRAME.

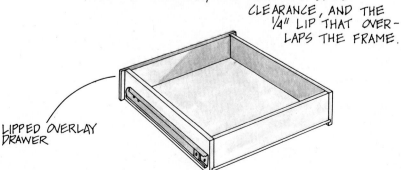

LIPPED OVERLAY DRAWER

Face Frames and Miter Boxes

Face Frames

Face frames add strength, rigidity, and durability to lumber and plywood cases alike; see the plywood case on page 75 for a typical application. You can mount doors on them, close drawers against them, nail trim into them, cover exposed plywood edges with them. Face frames have aesthetic merits as well. They add a crisp, finished line, and the stiles (uprights) and rails (cross pieces) give your case proportion and scale to suit the piece to its surroundings. In general, let the stiles be of equal width, the bottom rail wider, and the top rail narrower. A doweling jig, bar or face-frame clamps, and an electric drill are all the assembly tools you need.

To mount the assembled frame, scrape off all excess glue. Using glue and either bar clamps or finishing nails, fasten the frame to the case, squaring the case to the frame as you proceed. Set and putty nail heads. Scrape off excess glue and sand all surfaces flush; finish as desired.

Miter Boxes

A miter box is handy for crosscutting stock up to 6 inches wide for face-frame parts, trim, shelf edging, toe-boards, and other narrow pieces. The metal miter box makes a full range of angle cuts, from 90 degrees to 30 degrees; the wood box cuts either 90 degrees or 45 degrees. The box should be screwed or clamped down securely.

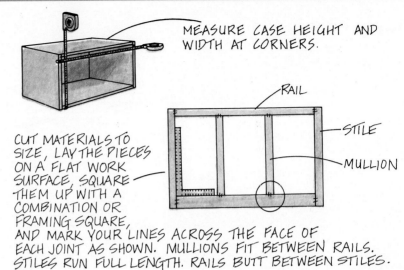

MEASURE CASE HEIGHT AND WIDTH AT CORNERS.

RAIL

STILE

MULLION

CUT MATERIALS TO SIZE, LAY THE PIECES ON A FLAT WORK SURFACE, SQUARE THEM UP WITH A COMBINATION OR FRAMING SQUARE, AND MARK YOUR LINES ACROSS THE FACE OF EACH JOINT AS SHOWN. MULLIONS FIT BETWEEN RAILS. STILES RUN FULL LENGTH. RAILS BUTT BETWEEN STILES.

USE A BIT SIZED TO YOUR JIG AND DOWELS AND DRILL THE HOLES A LITTLE DEEPER THAN HALF THE LENGTH OF THE DOWELS.

SQUIRT A BIT OF GLUE INTO EACH END GRAIN HOLE AND SPREAD SOME OVER THE END GRAIN ITSELF.

TAP GROOVED DOWELS IN TO HALF THEIR DEPTH; A BIT OF GLUE WILL EXIT. NOW SQUIRT A LITTLE GLUE INTO THE EDGE GRAIN HOLES AND ONTO SURFACES WHERE PIECES WILL MEET. (DON'T INSERT DOWELS.)

ASSEMBLE THE PIECES, AND TAP JOINTS SHARPLY WITH YOUR HAND TO SEAT. (OR, HAMMER JOINTS HOME, PROTECTING SURFACE WITH A SCRAP OF WOOD.)

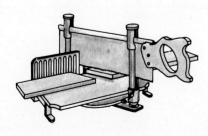

MEASURE DIAGONALLY TO CHECK FOR SQUARE. TO CORRECT IT, PUSH ABRUPTLY ON LONG CORNER UNTIL FRAME IS SQUARE.

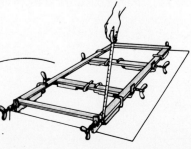

Hardware

Functioning Hardware

Hinges

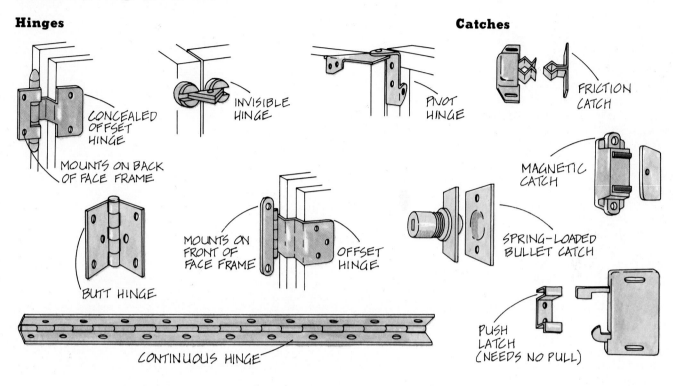

CONCEALED OFFSET HINGE

MOUNTS ON BACK OF FACE FRAME

INVISIBLE HINGE

PIVOT HINGE

BUTT HINGE

MOUNTS ON FRONT OF FACE FRAME

OFFSET HINGE

CONTINUOUS HINGE

Catches

FRICTION CATCH

MAGNETIC CATCH

SPRING-LOADED BULLET CATCH

PUSH LATCH (NEEDS NO PULL)

Pulls, Knobs, and Decorative Hardware

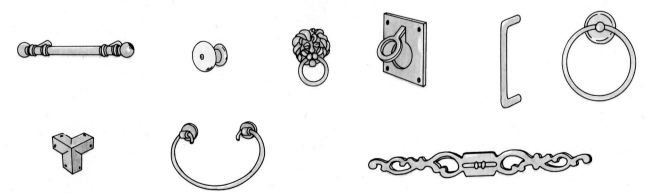

Installation Hardware

Wall Fasteners

Select wall fasteners according to your wall's construction. When you can locate studs, and they're just where you need them, fasten the work with screws. To fasten a project to the wall itself, use expansion shields or hollow-wall fasteners.

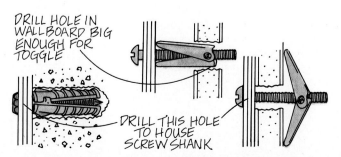

DRILL HOLE IN MASONRY JUST LARGE ENOUGH FOR ANCHOR

DRILL HOLE IN WALLBOARD BIG ENOUGH FOR TOGGLE

DRILL THIS HOLE TO HOUSE SCREW SHANK

Finishing

Scraping, puttying, and sanding initiate the finishing process. They don't require a lot of time, as long as you give the process some good, concentrated attention. The tone and quality of your finished product will reflect the care you take in preparing the surface for finishing.

Scraping

Scrapers clean off dried glue, bring face frames flush to case sides, remove saw marks and burns, and perform other presanding tasks. When the scraper stops bringing up frothy curls with each pass, it's time to sharpen it.

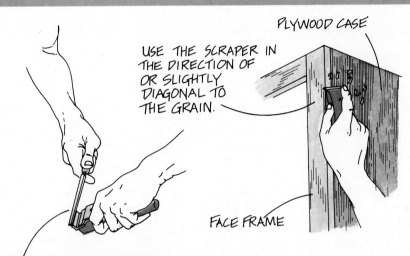

USE THE SCRAPER IN THE DIRECTION OF OR SLIGHTLY DIAGONAL TO THE GRAIN.

PLYWOOD CASE

FACE FRAME

Puttying

Wood putty fills voids, defects, gaps, and nail holes for surfaces on which you'll use a natural finish. Apply it with a flexible putty knife. Fast-drying putty, in a tone that matches your material, stains very well. Apply it sparingly and sand it thoroughly until no "ghosts" show around the puttied hole.

Spackling compound, rather than putty, is used for filling surfaces you plan to paint. For the best job, apply it right over the prime coat, when defects are most fully visible.

TO SHARPEN THE BLADE, PASS A FILE ACROSS IT A FEW TIMES IN ONE DIRECTION.

PUTTY SOMETIMES SHRINKS. TWO LIGHT APPLICATIONS MAY WORK BETTER THAN A SINGLE HEAVY ONE.

Sanding

You'll get the best results from sanding when you do the work in the proper sequence. Do inside surfaces once, before the parts are assembled, with medium fine sandpaper—120- or 150-grit, for example. When your construction is complete, putty outside surfaces as needed, then sand, completing the process with one grit before you graduate to the next finer.

SAND IN THE DIRECTION OF THE GRAIN. REMOVE CROSS-GRAIN SCRATCHES WITH A HANDBLOCK.

LIGHTLY BREAK THE EDGES WITH 150-GRIT ON A HANDBLOCK HELD AT ABOUT 45° TO THE WORK.

Wood Finish Processes

Belt sander. For early phases of the finishing process. Use grits from 80 to 120 for the initial sanding.

Electric vibrator sander. For middle to final finish. Orbital sanders in particular can go with and across the grain. Use grits from 120 up.

Hand block. For all phases of the finishing process. Use any grit.

Stained & Sealed Surfaces | | Primed & Painted Surfaces

For an All-Lumber Project		For an All-Lumber Project
1. 80 ● ■	smooths uneven surfaces, removes mill marks, removes surface putty and excess glue	**1.** 80 ● ▲
2. 120 ● ■	continues smoothing and evening-out process	**2.** 120 ● ▲
		3. Prime; fill imperfections with spackling compound when dry
	smooths raised grain and compound	**4.** 150 ● ▲
3. 180 ● ▲	prepares surface for finish	**5.** 180 ●
4. Apply first finish		**6.** Paint
5. 220 400 ● ▲	keeps surface smooth and even between coats	**7.** 180 ●
6. Reapply finish		**8.** Apply final paint coat

For a Plywood & Lumber Project		For a Plywood & Lumber Project
1. 100 ● ▲	smooths and evens surfaces	**1.** 80 ● ▲
2. 150 ● ▲	continues smoothing process, begins to prepare surface for finish coats	**2.** 120 ● ▲
		3. Prime; fill imperfections with spackling compound when dry
	smooths raised grain and compound	**4.** 150 ● ▲
3. 180 ● ▲	completes surface preparation for finish coats	**5.** 180 ●
4. Apply first finish coat		**6.** Paint
5. 220 400 ● ▲	keeps surface smooth and even between coats	**7.** 180 ●
6. Apply final finish coat		**8.** Apply a final paint coat

For a Particle Board Project		For a Particle Board Project
1. 100 ● ▲	smooths surface and edges (this is all the surface-preparation sanding you need do; particle board is rough, and more sanding will make little difference to the finish)	
	smooths surface	**1.** 120 ● ▲
2. Apply first finish coat		**2.** Prime; fill imperfections with spackling compound when dry
	smooths raised grain and compound and prepares surface for paint	**3.** 150 ● ▲
		4. Paint
3. 220 ● ▲	keeps surface smooth and even between coats	**5.** 180 220 ● ▲
4. Apply final finish coat		**6.** Apply final paint coat

METRIC CONVERSION CHART

U.S. MEASURE AND METRIC MEASURE CONVERSION CHART

		FORMULAS FOR EXACT MEASURE			ROUNDED MEASURES FOR QUICK REFERENCE				
	Symbol	When you know:	Multiply by:	To find:					
MASS (WEIGHT)	oz	ounces	28.35	grams	1 oz			=	30 g
	lb	pounds	0.45	kilograms	4 oz			=	115 g
	g	grams	0.035	ounces	8 oz			=	225 g
	kg	kilograms	2.2	pounds	16 oz	=	1 lb	=	450 g
					32 oz	=	2 lb	=	900 g
					36 oz	=	2¼ lb	=	1000 g (1 kg)
VOLUME	tsp	teaspoons	5	milliliters	¼ tsp	=	1/24 oz	=	1 ml
	tbsp	tablespoons	15	milliliters	½ tsp	=	1/12 oz	=	2 ml
	fl oz	fluid ounces	29.57	milliliters	1 tsp	=	1/6 oz	=	5 ml
	c	cups	0.24	liters	1 tbsp	=	½ oz	=	15 ml
	pt	pints	0.47	liters	1 c	=	8 oz	=	250 ml
	qt	quarts	0.95	liters	2 c (1 pt)	=	16 oz	=	500 ml
	gal	gallons	3.785	liters	4 c (1 qt)	=	32 oz	=	1 l
	ml	milliliters	0.034	fluid ounces	4 qt (1 gal)	=	128 oz	=	3¼ l
LENGTH	in.	inches	2.54	centimeters	⅜ in.	=	1 cm		
	ft	feet	30.48	centimeters	1 in.	=	2.5 cm		
	yd	yards	0.9144	meters	2 in.	=	5 cm		
	mi	miles	1.609	kilometers	2½ in.	=	6.5 cm		
	km	kilometers	0.621	miles	12 in. (1 ft)	=	30 cm		
	m	meters	1.094	yards	1 yd	=	90 cm		
	cm	centimeters	0.39	inches	100 ft	=	30 m		
					1 mi	=	1.6 km		
TEMPERATURE	F°	Fahrenheit	5/9 (after subtracting 32)	Celsius	32° F	=	0° C		
					68° F	=	20° C		
	C°	Celsius	9/5 +32	Fahrenheit	212° F	=	100° C		
AREA	in.²	square inches	6.452	square centimeters	1 in.²	=	6.5 cm²		
					1 ft²	=	930 cm²		
	ft²	square feet	929	square centimeters	1 yd²	=	8360 cm²		
					1 a	=	4050 m²		
	yd²	square yards	8361	square centimeters					
	a	acres	.4047	hectares					

Index

Acknowledgments

Photographic Locations

Diane Saeks
San Francisco, CA

Additional Photography

Page 15, left
Robert Perron
New York, NY

Designers

Page 10, top
Philip Emminger
Lafayette, CA

Pages 11, top; 20, left
David Lavrich
DLM Construction
San Francisco, CA

Pages 12, top; 13, right;
19, top; 21
Tony Pisacane
San Francisco, CA

Page 12, bottom left
Kitchen of
Anthony Dias Blue
Food Writer
San Francisco, CA

Page 12, bottom right
Ron Silberman
Fordham Park Construction
El Cerrito, CA

Page 15, left
Robert Nevins
Tucson, AZ

Page 15, right
Les Hack
San Francisco, CA

Pages 16, left and right;
22, top and bottom
Antonio F. Torrice
Just Between Friends
San Francisco, CA

Pages 18 and 19, bottom
Dan Phipps
Phipps and Tritt
San Francisco, CA

Page 21, right
Germano Milano
San Francisco, CA

Page 23, top
Stephen Shubel
San Francisco, CA

Page 23, bottom
Peter VanDine
Tanner & VanDine Architects
San Francisco, CA

Page 24, top
Penny Westphal
Lafayette, CA

Page 24, bottom, and 25
Lambert Woods Architects
San Francisco, CA

Special Thanks to:

Anthony Dias Blue
Conran's
Flax Office Supplies
Kit and Linda Hinrichs
Anna Korth
David and Mary Lavrich
Dan and Luciann Leraul
Marlene Levinson
S. Mannoff Showrooms, Ltd.
Mobilia
Tony Pisacane
Plus Kitchens
Lauren Poplack
Roche-Boboi's
Stephen Shubel
Evelyne Thomas
Tony Torrice
Dan and Sandra Webster
Roger and Penny Westphal

Product Manufacturers

Page 46
Cubes by Palaset

Page 48
Rollaround wire-mesh drawer unit
by Elfa/La; taboret by Boby.

Page 49
Stackable plastic baskets by
Ingrid Ltd.; cardboard files by
Esselte-Pendaflex.

Page 50
Wooden cutlery tray by Bartlett
Design & Manufacturing; wooden
rollout door-mount lazy Susan, and
rollout wire-mesh shelf and lid
rack by Amerock Corp.; stacking
plastic drawers and free-standing
lazy Susan by Rubbermaid; fabric-
covered jewelry trays by Lee/Rowan.

Page 51
Lazy Susan and wall-hung organizers
by Rubbermaid; under-shelf basket
by Heller Designs, Inc.; blade
stow by Cuisinart; hair-dryer and
cosmetic stows by Cosmepak, Inc.

Page 52
Wall hooks by Interdesign, The
Ironmonger, and Schulte Corp.

Page 53
Ironing center by Iron-A-Way Co.,
Inc.; wall-mounted grid by Heller
Designs, Inc.

Page 54
Closet shelving by Closet Maid;
plastic stacking drawers by A &
E products; door-back shelving
by Schulte Corp.

Page 55
Shoe bag by Patti Collins Canvas
Products; closet interior by
Just Closets; plastic boxes and
hangers by Lee/Rowan; plastic
drawer units by A & E Products.

Page 56
Armoire by Royal Country Classics.

Page 57
Wall system by Studimo; home
office by Link.

Technical Consultants

Bob Beckstrom
The Owner Builder Center
Berkeley, CA

Steve Crocker
Emminger Woodworking
and Construction
Lafayette, CA

Editorial Researchers
and Assistants

Nancy Cooney
Beverley DeWitt

Graphic Design Assistants

Kimiko Murakami
Mari Jo Whelan

Illustration Assistants

Margaret Best
Charles Fuhrman
Jayne Osgood
Connie Wharton

Copyediting and Proofreading

Editcetera
Berkeley, CA

Typesetting

George Lithograph
San Francisco, CA

Color Separation

Color Tech
Redwood City, CA